THE RECONSTRUCTION OF
THE CHURCH—
ON WHAT PATTERN?

THE RECONSTRUCTION OF THE CHURCH— ON WHAT PATTERN?

E. STANLEY JONES

ABINGDON PRESS

NASHVILLE   NEW YORK

CONTENTS

INTRODUCTION

This is my eighty-fourth birthday. I sit on a veranda in a valley of Mexico surrounded by mountains—I sit here between meetings while Spanish speakers hold forth in a YMCA camp where a Christian Ashram is being held. Before daybreak I was awakened by the sound of music. I thought at first it was a record being played over a loudspeaker. But I soon found it was not an impersonal, mechanical record being played, but a group of about thirty Spanish and North American Christians gathered in front of my door to serenade me with their hymns to congratulate me on my eighty-fourth birthday. Instead of it being mechanical music being played mechanically and impersonally—the word of music become word—it was the word of music become flesh, in gracious Latin American flesh.

Why should they congratulate me on being eighty-four? What was there in my having lived that long to make them happy and reverent? The Hindus think eighty-four is an especially auspicious age, for at eighty-four one has seen a thousand moons. So they said: "You must come back to India and let us celebrate especially that particular birthday." But to celebrate a birthday around the moon is to celebrate around the secondary, the moon is secondhand light, better than no light at all, but still the secondhand and of secondhand importance.

Did this group sing before daybreak because they and I were fellowshipping around the firsthand—around the sun, instead of the moon? Linyutang, the Chinese writer, in describing his return to Christ from secularism, put it in these words: "Put out the candles, the sun is up!" Did the group and Linyutang and I see that the only fellowship had to be around the firsthand, around the Sun, around Christ and not around the secondhand in the Christian faith—around minor issues?

Christianity is moonlight, secondhand, built up through the centuries; Christ is sunlight, firsthand, not built up through the centuries, but revealed from eternity—the revelation of the meaning of God and man and life. Our fellowship must be around the firsthand, around the sun, if it be real. Our fellowship must be around Christ—the firsthand.

Is all this irrelevant reverie, or do I come straight to the heart of the matter of the reconstruction of the church? I believe this is not reverie but revelation.

The church needs reconstruction—both friend and foe agree on that. "It is the depravity of institutions and movements that given in the beginning to express life they often end in throttling that very life. Therefore they need constant review, perpetual criticism, a continuous bringing back to original purposes and spirit." The Christian church is no exception. It is the chief illustration of the above.

I believe in the Christian church. It has been and is the mother of my spirit. At her altars I found Christ. The church brought me him—incomparably the most precious gift of my life. Three days ago I knelt at the spot where I first found him. (The church in moving to a larger church cut the altar rail and made a prayer desk out of it with the inscription on it: "At this place Stanley Jones knelt and gave himself to Christ," inviting others to do the same.) Periodically I kneel at this place and water it with my inner and outer tears of gratitude, the profoundest gratitude that nature is capable of.

With all its faults the church has been and is the greatest serving institution on earth. It has many critics but no rivals in the work of service to humanity. There isn't a spot on earth, from the frozen north to the tropical islands of the seas, where we haven't gone with schools, hospitals, leper, blind, and orphan asylums, and homes for the poor and the aged, churches, the Gospel—everything to lift the soul, the mind, the body of the human race. No other institution has done, or is doing, anything like it. The head of one of the new African governments said to me: "Where the Christian church is strong we have few problems. Where the church is weak or nonexistent we have nothing but problems."

But there is something deeper than the fruits of Christianity. Deeper than the fruits are the roots. An African chief in the Congo, asking for a "revival" for his village, said in making the request: "We are grateful for the fruits of the Christian faith—hospitals and education—but what we really need is the roots—changed character." That African chief with deep insight put his finger on the central need in East and West, North and South—the need for power to change character.

In the person of Jesus Christ the Christian church holds within itself a motive and power that does produce changed character. So Jesus Christ is the center of worth and hope of the Christian church. We have this treasure in an earthen vessel. Don't point to the earthen vessel—its cracks, its outworn inscriptions, its outworn shape, its unmodern appearance, but rather look at what it holds. It holds the person of Jesus Christ. As long as it holds him, it holds the most precious, the most potent, and the most present value that this universe holds, barring none. I say "present" for Jesus Christ is the Great Contemporary, and the Great Future. Everything and every person who departs from him decays and everything that comes to him and obeys him is resurrected, reconstructed, re-directed, redeemed, and revitalized. Again, no exception.

So this attempt to point to the pattern for the reconstruction of the Christian church will gaze at Jesus Christ and glance at the earthen vessel—the church which contains this Treasure. I will be critical, sometimes devastatingly critical, of the system built up around him, but as I do so, it will be with as much tenderness as I would point out the fading health on my mother's cheek. For the church is the mother of my spirit. When I point out its faults, I point out my own. For as the Moral Rearmament group often says: "He who points a critical forefinger at another points three accusing fingers at himself." For I am a part of the church—its values my values, its weaknesses my weaknesses, its sins my sins. I have spent half my life in striving to win men to Christ and the church, and the other half in trying to win the church to Christ. I cannot agree with Mahatma Gandhi, when, in his reply to the question: "What is the greatest enemy of Christ in India?" he replied: "Christianity." This is overstated, but there is enough truth in it to make it sting. Christianity, the system built up around Christ, is often the enemy, the worst enemy of Christ.

For instance, a billboard outside a church in our country reads: "This church is the only church authorized by God to represent Jesus Christ in the world." A woman left a will requesting that she be buried in a lot on the other side of the cemetery, away from her husband, because she loved her husband and didn't want to embarrass him when she was raised, when Jesus returned, and her husband would be left behind, because she belonged to one denomination, the chosen, and he belonged to another, the not-chosen. The system divided them in life and death.

If this is crude, how about this: Certain ministers have a valid ministry if hands of a certain type of bishops are laid upon them, and all other ministers who haven't had those hands laid on them are invalid, this apart from the character of the bishops laying on the hands and apart from the character and fruitfulness of the ministers upon whom the hands are laid. Did Jesus inaugurate that mechanism so foreign to his own spirit? He was vital hence valid; did he inaugurate a mechanism to produce a validity?

A woman said to me: "Everything is being integrated in America but, thank God, we still have our churches left." "Churches left"—outside human brotherhood.

All four of these are equally crude and equally unchristian. If Jesus were here he would say what he said to the people of the Temple: "Take these things hence. It is written, my house shall be the house of prayer for all nations, but you have made it a den of thieves." A den of thieves where you make the privileges which belong to all into the possession of some. In a museum in Turkey there is a stone, which was once in the Temple at Jerusalem, with this inscription on it: "Let no Gentile pass this place on pain of death." Jesus' eyes must have rested on those words when he said: "Take these things hence."

But Jesus is here. And he is saying to the temple of the church: "Take these things hence." This book is an interpretation of what he would point to when he says to the church of to-day: "Take these things hence." But while he would point to what should be taken out, this book will be more of an interpretation of what he would have us bring in to represent his spirit in this modern age.

Twelve hundred high school girls signed decision cards in one meeting in Japan. That gave us cause for rejoicing. But one decision card stood out in meaningfulness. One girl wrote on the back of her decision card: "I am 100% for Christ, but I am only 50% for the church." She saw the difference. The Christian church was not Christian—except partially, probably 50%. This book is an attempt to raise the percentage of Christ in the church. It will never be 100% Christian, for we have this treasure in earthen vessels.

But the alarming thing is that there is a demand and a tendency to reduce the percentage of Christ in the Christian church to make it more universal, to dilute it with the culture of the day, to secularize the church.

Now do not misunderstand me. The Christian faith is the most secular of religions. It is the one faith that believes in the material. When God created the earth he looked upon it and "saw that it was good"—the material was God-created and God-approved; and the center of that faith is "the Word become flesh." The spiritual was to function in material terms. We are not ghosts, disembodied spirits floating over the material world in disdain of that lower world of matter. We are embodied beings and unless we function in material terms we do not function. We repudiate the Greek conception of the spirit as good and the material as evil; they are two sides of one reality and must function as a unit.

The Kingdom of God is the most radical conception ever presented to the human race and it is the most secular—"may thy kingdom come and thy will be done on earth." It meant nothing less than the replacement of this present unworkable world order, founded on greed and selfishness and exploitation, with God's order founded on love and service and mutual aid. There is a tension set up between the two.

Now the demand is to let down that tension—to accept this secular order as the Kingdom of God. The "Secular City" is the Kingdom. In other words, the flesh has become the Word!

But the Secular City is a driven order, driven by the urge to succeed, to become rich, to add to accumulation, to increase secular desires and things; not to love your neighbor *as* you love yourself, but to use your neighbor *for* yourself. It is a driven order, driven by self-interest. The secular controls the spiritual, becomes the spiritual modified by the Christian faith at the edges. The secular controls the spiritual, becomes the spiritual modified by the Christian faith at the edges. The secular is in control.

In the view of secularism the Kingdom of God is not the doing of the will of God on earth as it is done in heaven; it is the acceptance of the secular city as the Kingdom.

And now they say that the church to be able to function within that Secular City must adopt its culture, its language and its outlook. I agree that those who are within the church must know the culture, the language and the outlook of the secular city, for it must know what we are speaking to and hence direct its message accordingly. But that we should adopt that culture, language, and outlook is quite another thing and quite a different thing. For the center of the culture of the Secular City is essentially and fundamentally self-regarding. It is a driven society, driven by pagan urges to get on, to succeed, to get ahead, to get status, to accumulate no matter what happens to the other person. It is softened at the edges by Christian attitudes and principles, but at the center it is anti-Christian. It makes itself God. Therefore, to adapt yourself to that secular society so wholeheartedly that this adaptation becomes an adoption, then this is a fatal abdication of the Christian faith in favor of paganism, whatever its name. For the Christian faith says that one must lose his life in a higher purpose and a higher will and then one will find it. This secular-city mentality and outlook says the opposite—find yourself by asserting and looking after yourself in every way possible, in every situation possible. Therefore, if the modern demand for adaptation means adoption we are lost. We must be in the secular society but not of it. We must love that secular society but we must love something higher and more supremely. To merge is to be submerged. And if we are submerged we have no message. To have a message is to be different, inwardly aloof, conscious that we have something to give. Jesus ate with publicans and sinners as one of them, but when he was challenged, he said that "they that are whole need not a physician but they that are sick." He was there as a physician not as a fellow patient. He was different—that difference made the multitude crowd about him to touch him and be made whole.

To be universal we do not have to be less Christian. For the truly Christian person is the most universal person in the world. He becomes more universal when he becomes more Christian.

If the church of this age marries the spirit of this age, then in the next generation it will be a widow. For this generation of secularism will be succeeded by another generation of secularism with its culture and its language and its outlook. For secularism has no fixed basis; it is the result of drives that ebb and flow and go the way of pressures.

We must be fixed to something universal and timeless. There are two things that are universal and timeless: reality and love. When you have reality and when you apply that reality by love you are universal and can speak to any age and are at home in any age and vital in any age.

But to ape an age to get that age is futile. This age of youth has an acute nose for unreality and when youth sense that you are using their language and dress and outlook to catch them, they turn from you as "a phony." The head of the Campus Crusade for Christ in Canada told me that they tried aping the young people to get them—adopting their language, their dress, and growing their beards. They found it a failure. The youth saw through it. The Campus Crusade for Christ gave up emphasis on costume and returned to the emphasis on Christ; gave up emphasis on "campus" and returned to conversion. Now they were back in their native element—not fish flopping on an alien shore, but fish back in their native element again, at home! Not playing a part, but natural.

When the nonviolent, noncooperation movement for independence for India was on, the wearing of white homespun and handwoven khadi dress was the sign of a nationalist, one who wanted independence for India and who said so by the wearing of khadi. I felt I must identify myself with the movement for independence. So I wore khadi in public meetings to give public addresses. It was politically dangerous, for I might be sent out of India by the British. I asked a missionary what he thought of my wearing khadi and he said: "I think it is appropriate—for it expresses your inward attitudes. You believe in India's independence and are saying so." So now that India has her independence I still wear khadi at the Ashram at Sat Tal. They now know that it not a pose, but a position. But if I had used khadi to curry favor with the nationalists they would have seen through it at once. The fact that the president of India asked me to contribute a chapter to the National Memorial Volume to Mahatma Gandhi on the centenary commemoration of his birth, 1968, is proof that the country accepted me as a real friend of India in spite of, and maybe, in the minds of many, on account of, the fact that I am an evangelist of the Good News of Jesus Christ. Perhaps they saw in him I have reality and I hope they see him applied in love.

Reality and love are the two sides of the master key that will unlock the door to any situation. In the reconstruction of the church we must have reality and we must apply it in love.

I

THE CENTRAL CRITICISM
OF THE CHURCH

A pastor said to me wistfully: "Do you think there will be a Christian church in existence in another generation?" And he said it seriously. There is no doubt that the church is under its severest fire—the severest fire in its long history, both from within the church and from outside. What is the center of that criticism?

It seems that the center of that criticism is this: the church is irrelevant. It is not related to the problems of the day. It is guarding values that are no longer valuable. It is not geared into the problems and issues of modern life. I once stood on a hill in Central India. On the top of that hill was a fort, guarded by soldiers in their long uniforms and holding pikes. Once the center of that feudal state that fort was relevant, it held the authority and power of the state within its four thick walls. But the center of power and authority had moved beyond those thick walls; it had moved up the valley with the center of the city. The center of authority and power was now in that secular city and not in that fort. The fort was high and dry—and irrelevant. But soldiers were still pompously guarding that irrelevance.

That, the critics say, is the picture of the church of today. It is high and dry—and irrelevant. It is not geared into the problems of the secular city. It is pompously guarding irrelevant values and issues.

This we deny straight off. The values which the church is guarding are not valueless and they are not irrelevant. They are the most precious values in human society today or any day. Those values may be covered up in irrelevant forms and archaic language, but stripped of those irrelevant forms and language, they are the most relevant and precious and valuable possessions ever granted to the human race. Without them that secular city becomes a beehive of industry, getting nowhere and stinging itself to death in its struggle for self-centered survival.

What are the values which the church is guarding? I would name six: First, the Kingdom of God; second, the person of Jesus Christ; third, the possibility of a new birth in this birth; fourth, the power of the Holy Spirit within, enabling men to live out dynamically this new life in the midst of society; fifth, a fellowship of believers in which these four values can be cultivated and a nucleus from which they can be propagated— a leaven within society—the church; sixth, service to all as the only method of greatness for all—"He that would be great among you shall be the servant of all." Note "servant of all," apart from birth and class and status and race. To be a servant of some doesn't make you great, except a great snob.

Let us look at these six values and evaluate them in the light of modern need. First, the Kingdom of God. Jesus put the Kingdom of God first—he "went out preaching the Gospel of the Kingdom of God." And he sent out his disciples preaching the "Gospel of the Kingdom of God." It is the only thing he ever called "the Gospel"—the Good News.

This is what the earthborn totalitarians are seeking for and don't know it. They are seeking something which will bring life into total meaning and total goal and bring compartmentalized and fragmented life into unity and value. But there is this difference between God's totalitarianism and man's earthborn totalitarianisms: if you obey man's totalitarianisms totally you find total bondage; if you obey God's totalitarianism totally you find total freedom. For the Kingdom is your homeland and when you find it you find yourself. "Seek first the kingdom and all these things will be added unto you"—including yourself and your freedom. The freest person, and persons, in this world are the people who obey these Kingdom laws written in themselves and in the scriptures and live by them. For they are inwardly structured for them. These laws then are a liberty, their fulfillment is the fulfillment of yourself.

The secular city needs nothing so much as it needs to obey some overall totalitarianism which coincides with what is written in the structure of its being and in the needs of their life. Otherwise the secular city must be ruled by an infinite diversity of laws covering all phases of personal and collective life with an infinite number of lawyers ready to show an infinite number of ways how those laws can be evaded. The result—chaos. But if you obey the Kingdom laws, the result—cosmos!

So the church holds the first value of an overall plan of life for the individual and society, God's plan in the Kingdom of God.

Second, the church holds within itself the value of the person of Jesus Christ. No other institution or movement specializes on the person of Jesus Christ. When the church is Christian it is Christ-ian. Its supreme emphasis is upon Christ. It may interpret him badly and illustrate him faintly, but he is there. And he is there redemptively, breaking through those imperfect interpretations and going beyond those faint illustrations. In him the church has a principle and power of revival and renewal. Every rediscovery and reemphasis on Jesus has brought and still brings revival and renewal. Every departure from him in thought or emphasis brings decay.

In himself Jesus illustrates the meaning and purpose of the Kingdom—he is its illustration. The Kingdom is Christlikeness of character universalized. He was and is the Kingdom. He used interchangeably "for my sake" and "for the kingdom's sake." In him the absolute order and the absolute person coincide. Not only does absolute goodness and love look out of his eyes, but absolute power. God not only redeems in terms of Christ. He rules in terms of Christ. I repeat: He is the Kingdom embodied and illustrated.

That does two things for my faith: it makes it both personal and social. Personal, in that when I have relationships with him I have relationships with a person; the relationships are personal and tender and intimate. I am not obeying an impersonal law; I am responding to a personal love. My code is now a character. I am constrained by personal love, and not merely restrained by impersonal laws. Again, it makes my faith social. For when I have relationships with him I have relationships with a social order embodied in him—the Kingdom. As the Kingdom has relationships to the total life, so belonging to that Kingdom I have relationships to the total life. So my faith is not now individual and now social, it is by its very nature both. So I'm not interested in an individual gospel or a social gospel. I'm interested in one gospel, one gospel that lays its hand on the individual will and says, "Repent, surrender, and be converted," and lays its hand on the collective will and says: "Repent, surrender, and be converted."

If Jesus puts together the individual and the social in a living blend, he also puts together humanism and divinity in a living blend. He was a human being. He faced life as a man, calling on no power not at our disposal for his own moral battle. He performed no miracles for himself. He prayed as you and I pray, facing God. He is so like me, I can almost put my hand on his shoulder and say, "Brother man." But when I'm about to do it I can't. For he steps on the other side—on the side of God and confronts me with an offer that no man dare offer another without blasphemy: "Come unto me, and I will give you rest." He is unlike me. He is like me and therefore my example. He is unlike me, therefore my redeemer. I need both. I need someone to show me how to live and I need someone to redeem me and give me power to live. I need an example and a redeemer. If he were a man and only a man, he could be only my example. If he were God and only God he could be only my redeemer. But I need both. He puts humanism and divinity together.

So the modern urge to concentrate on the human finds its fulfillment in him. Pilate said: "Behold the man." We can still say with emphasis, "Behold the man," for we see in him what real manhood, uncorrupted by evil, is like. And we can say: "Behold the God." For he is the revelation of what God is like and what man can be like. He is the God-Man. If you are a humanist alone you see corrupted human beings, hence a disappointment. Freud, a humanist, said: "With rare exceptions, all of my fellow beings are worthless." Looking at man through Jesus the man, I can say, "All of my fellow beings are worthful." So you cannot believe long in man unless you believe in something more than man, a something or someone that puts worth, meaning, value in man. The disciples told a blind man to shut up when the blind man called out to Jesus to have mercy on him. They were not interested in blind men until Jesus showed his interest: "Bring him to me." They immediately rushed to him and said: "Arise, he is calling you." They followed his interest. They were not interested in the blind man until Jesus was. Jesus the Divine has aroused more interest in the unwanted of the world than all the humanists put together.

But if the divine Son of God has created more interest in the human than any other, the human Son of Man has created more interest in the divine than any other. When he said: "He that hath seen me hath seen the Father," interest at once centered in the Father. To be the Father of such a Son is to be a different Father than the One the theologians and philosophers apart from Jesus have depicted. The highest the Hindu philosophers could say of God was "Neti, Neti"—"not that, not that." Looking into the face of Jesus one of his followers said, "God is love"—said it for the first time in human history. It is true that they said "God loves" as a stray description, but never before had they said "God is love" by his essential nature and could not do an unloving thing without violating his own nature.

So the God-Man has shown us, actually shown us in his own person, what God and man are like. This revelation of God and man is of infinite value to man struggling to know the meaning of this thing called life. That value the Christian church holds. Compared to that value the values which the secular city holds are valueless.

The third value the Christian church holds is the new birth. "Except a man be born from above he cannot see the kingdom of God." Here is a possibility of a new beginning. When this birth in which we are living has been messed up (and for whom has it not been messed up?), then there is the possibility of a new birth in this birth, the Gospel of another chance, a fresh beginning. Where there is such a hope and such a possibility in any civilization as a new birth, moral and spiritual decay may be arrested and a new era begun. Without that possibility of a new birth in the individual and in society, sure decay sets in and death results.

But to have moral power to take hold of a crisis and turn the crisis to a higher life requires new birth in the individual and in society. Wherever that possibility is lacking there is sure decay and death. So moral and spiritual new birth, which the builders of modern civilization have rejected, has now become the head of the corner, the supreme necessity of modern life. Our intelligence has outrun our character. We have more power than moral character to handle that power. Because of that lack we may destroy ourselves by the very instruments which intelligence has created.

So Jesus sounds the cry across the face of the chaos of modern civilization: "Except a man (or a civilization) be born from above he cannot see the kingdom of God." Nothing, absolutely nothing, is more necessary in modern life in East or West, than to be born again. This value—the value of a possibility—and the actuality, of a new birth which the Christian church holds within itself in the person of Christ, is now the supreme value in human society. Unless man can be born again it is better that man had not been born. For without that new birth man is in imminent danger of self-destruction. With the new birth man can go anywhere he ought to go.

The fourth thing the Christian Church holds within itself as a supreme value in human living is the power of the Holy Spirit. I can see the eyebrows of this intellectually conscious age go up in surprise. But they will stay up there in fuller surprise when we look at the facts.

Man has desires to be good. Even the worst man puts on a frontage of goodness, meaning, "Goodness is good, and badness is bad, and I would like to be known as good to myself and others." He is not only convinced that the good is good but also that the good is good for me. Then why isn't he good? Because man hasn't power to put into action his innate desires for goodness. He is wicked because he is weak. His drives are too strong for him. Most of those drives could be summed up as three; they are in the subconscious—self, sex, and the herd. For his own moral and spiritual and social development man needs nothing so much as he needs some power that will cleanse these drives in the subconscious, coordinate and consecrate them. If, as Freud says, life is determined by urges in the subconscious, then nothing is more necessary than a power which can and does work redemptively in the subconscious and releases us from tensions between the conscious and the subconscious, unifying us there and making us free to develop and to be what we are made to be. This power is the Holy Spirit. The Holy Spirit is the applied edge of redemption, applied where we are most helpless, in the subconscious. For the area of the work of the Holy Spirit is largely in the subconscious mind. With our consent and cooperation the Holy Spirit works miracles where we stand helpless and baffled and beaten. We literally cannot control the subconscious by our willpower, our intellectual power, and by our emotional power, all combined. That seething caldron of desires in the subconscious will only obey the Spirit who moved upon the face of chaos in the beginning and out of which came cosmos. The Holy Spirit is nothing less than God breaking in, where invited, upon his process of evolution with adequate power and resources to produce a hastened evolution, a miracle of evolution, where it is needed most—in the subconscious. We are no longer suppressing these subconscious desires in the name of morality; we are expressing these subconscious desires on a higher level as creative activity. That step upward from a suppressed subconscious on a lower level to an expressed subconscious on a higher level is the most important moral and spiritual step ever made by man in his long history. Here he steps into a new freedom, the freedom to be, to create, and to live masterfully, without strain and without drain. A new and superior type of human being emerges, born from above.

So the stone, the Holy Spirit, which the builders of civilization have rejected has now become the head of the corner. Has become the deepest necessity of human living—the necessity to convert the subconscious from a warring enemy to a creative friend and ally.

That is a valuable value and only the church holds it, for it came through Jesus, the source and pattern and illustration of the spirit-controlled life. And he is incomparably the greatest person that ever lived on this planet. "Behold the man!"

The fifth value held by the Christian church is a fellowship of love in which these four values can be obtained, cultivated, and illustrated, a nucleus from which they can be propagated, a leaven within society.

If the Christian church were wiped out today you would have to create something like it to meet certain basic human needs. Man is a social being. To be is to be in relations. Therefore, the church exists to meet that social need. The Christian life cannot be lived in solitude. Someone asked the superintendent of a mental institution why they had so few guards. The reply: "The insane never organize. They are entirely individualistic." So the church, when it is a real church, is a society of organized love. It teaches young and old to live together as members of a society that cares, cares for everybody everywhere. The Christian church is the one organization dedicated not to itself but to others. A little boy of six and a little girl of five came across the dining room hand in hand at one of our Ashrams. The little boy asked if they might ask a question: "What is the Christian attitude?" I thought I had misunderstood him so I asked him to repeat the question, which he did. I replied: "Well, I suppose the Christian attitude is to love everybody, everywhere." He thought a moment, nodded his head in approval, and they went back across the room hand in hand. Six and five! To drop that into the consciousness of children of six and five with approval is an invaluable value. Among Americans as a whole, there is one divorce in four marriages; among church members, one in fifty; among those who pray and read their Bibles in family prayers, one in five hundred. Evidently exposure to God and Christ in prayer in a family circle, plus the fellowship of the church, makes for family stability, a great asset to society. Without the church fellowship and family praying, life tends to be centrifugal, with it life tends to be centripetal. In Christ "all things cohere," hold together. Outside of Jesus Christ all things are incoherent, they fall apart.

Sixth, greatness through service is the most constructive drive ever introduced into human nature. It ennobles those to whom it is directed and it ennobles the one who serves. Nothing is such an all-around ennoblement as greatness through service to all.

We now turn to see what further values the church holds beyond the six mentioned, values which no other organization or movement holds, except as they have taken them over consciously or unconsciously from the church.

When Jesus said simply to his disciples, "Now you are clean through the word which I have spoken to you," the whole history of civilization was wrapped up in that statement. By his teaching and actions and attitudes he had cleansed them and their universe. First, he cleansed their universe from many gods and goddesses and gave them one God, our heavenly Father. In India there were supposedly 330,000,000 gods, almost a god to a man. Think of what it meant to the unity of the human race to cleanse away those competing gods and goddesses and bring us into the conception and fact of one God, our heavenly Father, and men therefore our human brothers, one family under one God. Nothing, absolutely nothing has done so much as that to unify humanity.

Second, he cleansed the character of the one God, and turned him from an irresponsible autocrat into one whose nature is love and who is great because he is the servant of all and is Christ-like in character. That is important for "show me your gods and I will show you your men." Now there is nothing higher in God or man than to be Christlike.

Third, he cleansed greatness: "the greatest among you shall be the servant of all." No longer is the man great who has a great number of servants, but that man is great who serves the greatest number.

Fourth, he cleansed the home from being a harem, made it into a home where one man and one woman live together till death parts them, physical death, or moral death. He thus laid the most solid foundation for human society ever laid. All else is sand; this is rock.

Fifth, he cleansed the relations between persons: "Thou shalt love thy neighbor as thyself"—not less than yourself, not more, but "as," making self-love and other-love equal.

Sixth, he cleansed the earth from being "Maya," illusion, into being the scene of the coming of the Kingdom of God: "May thy kingdom come and thy will be done on earth as it is in heaven." The earth has a destiny—the Kingdom of God is to come on it.

Seventh, he cleansed the conception of the future of the earth and the future of man from fragmentation and meaninglessness by making that future, and this present, to come under one total order, the Kingdom of God. That conception gives total meaning and total goal to all life, material and spiritual. This gives us God's totalitarianism to offset and make unnecessary man's earthborn totalitarianism, fascism, naziism, and communism.

Eighth, he cleansed the Greek idea of the material being evil and the spiritual being good. The material was to be the agent of the spiritual: "And the Word was made flesh," both spiritual and material, two sides of one reality, both can be dedicated and used of God.

Ninth, the body is sacred, if dedicated: "You are God's temple."

Tenth, he cleanses prayer as a mechanism for getting boons out of God and turned it into surrender to the will of God, made it a communion and a cooperation.

Eleventh, he cleansed love from *eros*, possessive love, into *agape*, self-giving love, and made this cleansed love into life's highest value and commandment, love to God and love to man.

Twelfth, he cleansed away a guilt-ridden life of self-condemnation and offered men a new birth in this birth, a clean slate and a fresh beginning.

Thirteenth, he cleansed the future life from a life of "horis" and "shades" and made it into a heaven of growth and development, the finite infinitely approaching the infinite but never becoming the infinite, the whole ending in communion, but never union. We never become God.

Fourteenth, he cleansed union with God and saved it from submergence into the divine: "You in me and I in you"—the "I in you" saves our personality and adds a plus to it, so that Christ-realization produces self-realization.

Fifteenth, he cleanses us from escapism and gives us power, not merely to bear trouble and sorrow and injustice and unmerited suffering, but to use it, to take it up into the purpose of our lives and make it contribute. He took the worst thing that could happen to him, namely, his crucifixion, and turned it into the best thing that could happen to the world, its redemption. Professor William James says "This positive active way of dealing with sorrow gives a new dimension to life." You can live *in spite of* when you can't live *on account of*.

Sixteenth, he cleanses high standards from futility and discouragement by providing power to realize those goals, the power of the Holy Spirit. The Holy Spirit is the applied edge of redemption, applied in the subconscious mind where we need power to control the driving urges of self, sex, and the herd, which reside in the subconscious. The subconscious can be redeemed and redirected and made spiritually fruitful.

Seventeenth, he cleansed religious demands and burdening rites and ceremonies and reduced them to simplicity: "Called to belong to Jesus Christ." (See Rom. 1-6 RSV.) Psychology points to basic human needs: The need to belong, the need for significance, the need for reasonable security. The Christian faith points beyond the vague belonging of psychology to the One to whom we should belong: "Called to belong to Jesus Christ." The doing and the being come out of the belonging.

Eighteenth, he cleansed life from being a joyless journey and set it to music: "That my joy may be in you and that your joy may be full."

Nineteenth, he cleansed life from itself as a burdensome pessimism and said: "I have come that you might have life and that you might have it more abundantly." The answer to life was more life, abundant life, inner adequacy within to meet anything that could happen on the without. We love life because we love Life.

Twentieth, Jesus made these nineteen things possible by giving himself on a cross to make all these things actual. He gave promise and gave commandment, then he gave himself, gave himself on a cross. There he bore our sins in his own body, became sin for us. Then he rose again from the dead. All the values he gave he shows are alive, alive in him. The good is not only good, it is triumphant, alive forever more, in him!

Here in these twenty things Jesus Christ introduces us into the cleanest and most desirable universe, within and without, ever presented to the human race, anywhere, at any time and presents himself as its illustration and embodiment. If the Christian church holds within itself Jesus Christ in a living way, it holds the greatest values ever received by man in all his long journey upward. I say "received" and not "conceived" by man for man could not and did not conceive it, it is a stark gift of God.

To listen to a confused and tangled age, confused and tangled by its own revolt against these values, and to accept even in thought that the above values are irrelevant is to be the modern Esau who sells his birthright for a mess of modern pottage. I inadvertently left my New Testament in a vacant seat on a plane a few days ago in Latin America. It was well-marked with many marginal notes gleaned from many hours of meditation. It was precious in itself and more precious for what I had added. The clean-up squad apparently picked up the newspapers and the New Testament and threw them out together on the refuse dump. That is the moral equivalent of the modern age in throwing out the New Testament and classifying it as on the same level of worth as an outdated daily newspaper. The one is outdated almost before the ink is dry and the other is the most precious heritage of the human race, ageless and deathless and priceless.

We note, in passing, the almost pell-mell inclination in some circles to make the pattern for reconstruction of the church "the secular city," everything must be "secular." In the great world missionary conferences of 1928 and 1938, secularism was the archenemy of Christianity in the world, far more serious than the non-Christian religions systems. For secularism said that the only values are material values, the only realities are the material realities. This was looked on as Enemy number One. Now this is changed. Now the only values are secular values; the secular is the sacred. It is true a distinction is made between secularism and secularization, secularism is good and secularization is bad. But this is an artificial distinction, a distinction without a difference.

So everything Christian has to be made into the secular to prove its validity. We have "The Secular Congregation," "The Secular Saint," even "The Secular Christ." This is a symptom of the fading out of the spiritual and the emerging of the secular as the only reality. It is a symptom of humanism replacing Christian values. This secular humanism is a one-sided interpretation of life. In the face of this a scientist, A. Cressy Morrison, says: "No atom or molecule ever had a thought, no combination of the elements ever gave birth to an idea, no natural law ever built a cathedral; but obedient to certain impulses of life, certain living structures have been made which contain something to which the particles of matter, are, in turn, obedient, and we see as a result the wonders of civilization. What is this living structure? Atoms and molecules? Yes, and what else? An intangible something so superior to matter that it dominates all things, and so different from the material that it cannot be seen, weighed or measured. . . . The soul of man is master of its destiny but is conscious of the relation to the supreme source of its destiny." While religious people are going over pell-mell to prove the Christian faith is secular the scientists are saying the above, namely, that there is "an intangible something so superior to matter that it dominates all things."

The pendulum swings from an age which said that the spiritual is everything and the secular or material is nothing to the other side, which says that the secular is all and the spiritual is nothing. In both cases it is like a bird trying to fly with one wing, instead of flying it goes around in circles. This revolt from the spiritual to the secular is clearly an attempt to fly with one wing. There will be a revolt from this lopsided interpretation of life as material to one that considers life as spiritual and material. Then we will take off with two wings and soar. Now we are going round in circles.

This secularism says there is one commandment: "Thou shalt love thy neighbor as thyself," trying to fly with one wing, going around in circles. The Christian faith has two wings: "Thou shalt love the Lord thy God" and "Thou shalt love thy neighbor as thyself." When these two are equally emphasized, the Christian faith soars.

This bothness is seen in John 3:16: "God so loved the world, that he gave his only begotten Son, that whosoever believes in him shall not perish but have eternal life." This was the chief emphasis in previous generations, one wing procedure, going in circles. Now we see 1 John 3:16 as its other wing: "It is by this that we know what love is: that Christ laid down his life for us. And we in our turn are bound to lay down our lives for our brothers." If John 3:16 was the chief emphasis of a generation ago, the emphasis on what God has done; now this generation is adopting 1 John 3:16 as its golden text. They are both needed if we are to cease going round in circles.

In the early church were two communions, the Lord's Supper and the Love Feast; one signifying what Christ has done for us upon the cross and the other signifying that in this Love Feast they were eating a common bread, were distributing their wealth to the needy, they had all things in common. But it was easier to celebrate the Holy Communion, or what he did for us, than it was to maintain the Love Feast, or what we are to do for the needy, so the Love Feast dropped out. Christianity is trying to fly with one wing, celebrating the communion with his self-giving and neglecting or refusing to eat the bread of the Love Feast, a communion with our brothers in need.

So we do not work from a religious relativism, or secularistic religion, to a relativism, or unalloyed secularism—from a relativism to a relativism. We work from an absolute, the Kingdom of God on earth, to a relativism, secularism.

We are Christians, not secularists. We work from Christ down and he worked from the Kingdom of God down, "He went out preaching the gospel of the kingdom," himself the meaning and illustration of that kingdom. He used interchangeably "for my sake" and "for the Kingdom's sake."

We wince when we find Christians divided into "pietists and secularists," as one book puts it. I do not want to be a pietist or a secularist, loathesome names. I want to be a Christian. Nor do I want the Christian church reconstructed into the image of the pietists or the image of the secularists. I want it to be Christian.

Jesus said: "Beware of the leaven of Pharisees and the Sadducees." The Pharisees were the outwardists, having the hypocrisy of the outer without the inner; but the Sadducees were the secularists. Jesus warned against both. That double warning is needed today.

The Christian, when truly Christian, is the most universal man in the world. By his very nature as a Christian he must be a universal man, for he follows the universal Son of man.

When I asked Mahatma Gandhi, in 1919, what we Christians should do to make Christianity more naturalized in India, not a foreign thing identified with a foreign country and a foreign government, but naturalized and contributing its power to India's uplift and redemption, he replied straight off: "I would suggest four things: First, that all of you Christians, missionaries and all, must begin to live more like Jesus Christ. Second, that you practice your religion without adulterating it or toning it down. Third, that you emphasize love and make it your working force, for love is central in Christianity. Fourth, that you study the non-Christian religions more sympathetically so that you can have a more sympathetic approach to the people." Now note: Three out of the four suggestions about naturalizing the Christian faith in India emphasized the three things in the Christian faith; namely, the person of Jesus Christ as the center and the center of the manifestation of faith is to live more like him; that you practice your faith in him without toning him down, or adulterating the faith built up around him. In other words, you will not universalize your faith by introducing into it foreign elements such as secularism, or other passing fads; practice it as is, for by its very nature it is universal.

Then add to this amazing tribute to the universality of the Christian faith the suggestion of making "love your working force, for love is central in Christianity." But note that earlier we made love one of the two elements which are always universal and relevant, namely reality and love. Here the Mahatma emphasized both, the reality of Christ, without being toned down or adulterated, and this reality worked out into life through love. Could anything be more explicit and important?

But this is not a chance statement, given politely by the great-souled Gandhi. It was a considered conclusion. The same conclusion came out of Japan. When a committee was appointed to bring in a report on how to make Christianity more naturalized in Japan, with a professor of Japanese culture as the head of it, we would have thought they would have suggested that the Christian faith should be adulterated with Japanese culture and thought to make it universal. They didn't. The substance of the report could be summed up in two words: "Be Christian."

May I add another from a Jewish Rabbi? When I sat down alongside him after a Rotary Club address I asked, "Rabbi, was I too Christian for you in that address?" "Oh, no," he replied, "for the more Christian you are, the better you will treat the Jews."

Here we find three voices, one from India, one from Japan, one from the Dispersion, all saying the same things: "If you want to be universal and valid for today: Be Christian."

May I add another, this time from a secularist multimillionaire: "If Brother Stanley can't convert me, I will sue him." This was said half jokingly and half seriously, but it is what the world is half saying and sometimes wholly thinking: "If you Christians can't convert us, we will sue you for breach of promise." You promised this, now fulfill it. Boiled down to its essence, this is the core of the criticism of the church: "Show that you can and will convert us or we will sue you for breach of promise." For mind you there is no real promise of hope from any direction except the church of Jesus Christ, if that church is truly Christian.

So we turn to see if the church has a pattern for reconstruction, a pattern of its own. If it takes its pattern from a secular world it will be an echo and not a voice. Jesus said of the religious leaders of the day: "You must not copy them" (Matt. 7:8, Moffatt). And further he said: "No man putteth a piece of new cloth into an old garment." (Matt. 9:16 KJV). Modern secularism is the old garment of secularism that has come down through the ages. It is more polished and shining and brilliant, but down underneath it is the same selfish struggle for position and power and possessions. The struggle is more civilized, but it is more intensified by the mechanical power at our disposal, its essential nature is unchanged. So if the church tries to sew its new cloth of the Kingdom on the old garment of secularism it will make the rent worse, for the two just don't fit.

But—and this is the point—anything good in the old garment of secularism will not be destroyed but fulfilled: "I came not to destroy but to fulfill." But in the fulfilling of an old system Jesus destroys it by fulfilling it. He takes the good out of it, fulfills it in the Kingdom, and the bad which was a parasite on the good drops away like a shell when the kernel of the good is fulfilled in the Kingdom. That is revolution par excellence; it destroys a system as a system by taking out the good and fulfilling it, and thus rendering the old unnecessary and irrelevant, not capable of surviving. It was the good that made it survive. Jesus fulfills that good and thus makes the remaining system useless.

Thus Jesus will destroy communism by fulfilling the two things that make it float, namely, a just distribution of goods for all, especially for the workers, and a wider contribution according to ability, both of which are inherent in the Christian faith ("distribution was made according to each one's necessities" and "if a man will not work neither shall he eat.") These are fulfilled in the Kingdom, but then the evil built up around this kernel of good—force, hate, atheistic materialism, and world domination—will drop away incapable of surviving. Nothing to hold it together.

So we must now turn to see what the Christian pattern for reconstruction is.

II

THE RECONSTRUCTION
OF THE CHURCH—
AFTER WHAT PATTERN?

While the center and core of our faith, Jesus Christ, is "the same yesterday and today and forever," the system built up around him must be subject to change. Otherwise it becomes the constrictive band around mummied forms. Fortunately, the Christian faith holds a Christ who is both static and dynamic. Static in that he is fixed in history and dynamic in that he moves beyond that history, fixed and unfolding. "I have yet many things to say to you, but you cannot bear them now. When the Spirit of truth comes, he will guide you into all the truth." (John 16:12-13 RSV.) Here he provided for a fixed but unfolding revelation. In this book we will endeavor to see if we can unfold that unfolding revelation, at least find the lines of development which the Christian movement holds within itself. The two guidelines holding us to that unfolding revelation are reality and love; the embodiment of both is Christ. We will gaze at him and glance at the secular city. We know that gazing at him we will be guided into the heart of the needs of the secular city. In gazing at him we will be saved from bewildering bypaths of minor and irrelevant issues.

I believe that the Christian church has its own pattern for reconstruction. And that the church at Antioch is that pattern. It was no mere chance that "in Antioch the disciples were for the first time called Christians" (Acts 11:26 RSV). They gave names in those days according to characteristics. If the characteristics changed, the name was changed. Jesus gave James and John the name of Boanerges ("sons of thunder") to remind them what they had been, tempestuous; he gave Peter the name of Cephas ("a rock") to remind him of what he expected him to be. Barnabas, before he surrendered his all to Christ, was named Joseph (literally "one more") probably because he belonged to a large family, and when they got down to him they ran out of names. But Joseph was not "one more," adding one to the statistics after he surrendered his all to Christ; he was a whole multiplication table, so they named him Barnabas, "son of consolation," or "son of encouragement." He didn't add, he multiplied! When the people looked at the group at Antioch they saw that the spirit of Christ had come to embodiment; since the group's central characteristic was Christ, they called them "Christ-ians." Christianity had come to its own—it was Christ-ian. That was no mere chance. It was Christ-ian.

Christianity did not come to its own in Jerusalem for two reasons: it was too racial and too authoritarian. The grave clothes of Judaistic outlook and customs were still clinging to the movement. The Jews tried to enforce their outlooks and customs on the Gentile converts. They even tried to invade Antioch with them; Paul had to withstand them. It meant jamming the Gospel back into a Jewish mold. The second reason that Christianity could not come into its own in Jerusalem was the fact that the Apostles made all the decisions and handed them down. The laity were on the edges or stifled. They had to be persecuted to Antioch to come to their own. There they did. The Christian Gospel was free to express its very nature and purpose at Antioch. The matrix of Jerusalem was too narrow (Jewish racialism) and too high (too authoritarian) to be universalized. The Christian movement had to be put into a new matrix, Antioch, to come to its own.

The tragedy of the Christian movement is that for the most

part it has through the centuries been centered in Jerusalem. The church has tried to be an "Apostolic Church." The church is not an apostolic church—it is not centered in the apostles, it is centered in Christ—it is a *Christian* church. Because the Christian church has, for the most part, centered in Jerusalem, there have been claims and rival claims about apostolic authority. I have no interest in apostolic authority. Our faith does not go back to the apostles, it goes back to Christ. The apostles were men, imperfect men like ourselves, and were never intended and never fitted to be the center of our faith. Only divine shoulders can bear that responsibility, Jesus Christ.

There is one passage which has been appealed to corroborate this apostolic centering: "laid upon the apostles and the prophets." But the New English Bible pulls out that one single possibility to found the church on the apostles and makes it read: "laid *by* the apostles and prophets", (Eph. 2:20 NEB). That brings the whole New Testament in line with Paul's statement: "There can be no other foundation beyond that which is already laid; I mean Jesus Christ himself" (1 Cor. 3:11, NEB). "No other foundation"—the attempt to build the Christian church on apostolic foundation is "another foundation," and hence not Christian. It has led to endless confusion and strife, and still does. We are centered in Christ; the terminus of our faith is Christ, not the apostles. To stop at the apostles for authority is to stop this side of Christ and therefore to stop this side of being Christian. When Jesus said: "You have heard it was said of old time, but I say unto you," he pointed to the past, making his own word final even in the Scriptures of the past. But he is saying still: "You have heard it said in after years, but I say unto you." All Scripture before and after Jesus Christ must come to the bar of his person for corroboration. If it fits his spirit it is Christian, if it departs from that spirit it is not Christian. Christianity is Christ.

We find our unity in Christ, not in the apostles. If we try to find our unity in the apostles we will be forever divided. If we find it in Christ we will be forever united. We have a saying in the Ashrams: "If you belong to Christ and I belong to Christ, we belong to each other." It is as simple as that and as profound.

When groups in Corinth began to say: "I belong to Paul," "I belong to Apollos," "I belong to Cephas," Paul protested that the allegiance was all wrong, that these apostles belonged to them—"all things belong to you, Paul, Apollos, Cephas, all great teachers. But you don't belong to them, anything good they have is yours, but you belong to Christ." Here Paul broke the nexus of loyalty to men and fastened it on Christ, one of the most important things that has happened in Christian history. He was saying in essence: Glance at men and gaze at Christ, that is Christian. But if you glance at Christ and gaze at men, it is sub-Christian. This centering of loyalty and building-up of doctrines on men is divisive, ever has been and ever shall be. This refers to the Roman Catholics' centering on Peter, the Lutherans' centering on Luther, the Calvinists' centering on Calvin, the Wesleyans' centering on Wesley, the Barthians' centering on Barth, the Bultmannians' centering on Bultmann and the Tillichites' centering on Tillich—they all alike divide. But when you center on Christ, that unites. If I were to say: "What do you believe?" any group will go apart, no two believing exactly alike. But if I were to say: "Whom do you trust?" all will come together—one name upon our lips, one loyalty in our hearts, Christ!

So the church at Antioch is a Christ-ian church and therefore has within it universal elements which can be, and are, valid for today and as up-to-date as tomorrow morning.

Before we analyze the elements in the Antioch church which apply for today, let us read the account given in Acts 11:19-30 and 13:1-3 NEB.

Meanwhile those who had been scattered after the persecution that arose over Stephen made their way to Phoenicia, Cyprus, and

Antioch, bringing the message to Jews only and to no others. But there were some natives of Cyprus and Cyrene among them, and these, when they arrived at Antioch, began to speak to Gentiles as well, telling them the good news of the Lord Jesus. The power of the Lord was with them, and a great many became believers, and turned to the Lord.

The news reached the ears of the church in Jerusalem; and they sent Barnabas to Antioch. When he arrived and saw the divine grace at work, he rejoiced, and encouraged them all to hold fast to the Lord with resolute hearts; for he was a good man, full of the Holy Spirit and of faith. And large numbers were won over to the Lord.

He then went off to Tarsus to look for Saul; and when he had found him, he brought him to Antioch. For a whole year the two of them lived in fellowship with the congregation there, and gave instructions to large numbers. It was in Antioch that the disciples first got the name of Christians.

During this period some prophets came down from Jerusalem to Antioch. One of them, Agabus by name, was inspired to stand up and predict a severe and world-wide famine, which in fact occurred in the reign of Claudius. So the disciples agreed to make a contribution, each according to his means, for the relief of their fellow-Christians in Judaea. This they did, and sent it off to the elders, in the charge of Barnabas and Saul to the elders.

There were at Antioch, in the congregation there, certain prophets and teachers: Barnabas, Simeon called Niger, Lucius of Cyrene, Manean, who had been at the court of Prince Herod, and Saul. While they were keeping a fast and offering worship to the Lord, the Holy Spirit said, 'Set Barnabas and Saul apart for me, to do the work to which I have called them.' Then, after further fasting and prayer they laid their hands on them and let them go.

Someone has said that Mary's song at the announcement of Jesus' birth has enough dynamite in it to blow our present world order to pieces. Well, this simple account of the church at Antioch has enough constructive revolutions in it to remake the present structure of the church of the world. Touch it anywhere and it pulsates with vitality, and not ancient but up-to-date vitality for now. It is real and therefore universal and applicable for now.

First of all, the church at Antioch was founded by laymen. The apostles at Jerusalem had nothing to do with the founding and carrying on of this church. It is true that after they heard of the marvellous grace manifested on the church at Antioch they sent Barnabas down to help them. But Barnabas was a layman. Paul too came later, but Paul also was a layman. So it was a lay church in its founding and in carrying on and in spreading through that whole ancient world. The account says of the persecution which arose over Stephen: "This was the beginning of a time of violent persecution for the church in Jerusalem; and all except the apostles were scattered over the country districts of Judea and Samaria." (Acts 8:1 NEB). I have often wondered why the apostles were not scattered with the rest of the church. Were they braver? I have come to the conclusion that in the eyes of the authorities they were less dangerous than the lay group, less dangerous for they fitted into the Jewish scheme of life better, were more Jewish. It was the lay group headed by Stephen who were the dangerous group, dangerous to the Jewish hierarchy, for they attacked the temple. The apostles attended it. Did not Stephen say:

However, the Most High does not live in houses made by men, as the prophet says: 'Heaven is my throne and earth my footstool. What kind of a house will you build for me, says the Lord; where is my resting place? Are not all these things of my own making?'

How stubborn you are, heathen still at heart and deaf to the truth! You always fight against the Holy Spirit.' . . . This touched them on the raw and they ground their teeth with fury. (Acts 7:48-54 NEB).

He had attacked them and their temple. This was dangerous, so Stephen was stoned. And the persecution fell upon the lay side of the movement. They embodied the revolutionary side of the Christian movement, its cutting edge. The apostles embodied the accommodating edge, so they were left alone.

It is true that the persecution later struck the apostles—James was beheaded and Peter thrown in prison. But the initial reaction was against the laymen; the fury fell upon them. Then the apostles were caught in the later mopping-up of the persecution carried on by King Herod because "he saw that the Jews approved." It was a side thrust of the spear of persecution; the main thrust was against the lay movement, the embodiment of disruptive principles and practices and very aggressive evangelism.

The account says, in regard to the lay movement that resulted in the founding of the church at Antioch, "Meanwhile those who had been scattered after the persecution that arose over Stephen made their way to Phoenicia, Cyprus and Antioch." These lay disciples instead of going underground went overland, "bringing the message." The persecution instead of stopping them, furthered them; they didn't bear it, they used it.

One of the least noticed and most important things about Stephen was his speech before the Sanhedrin, the longest recorded speech in the New Testament next to the Sermon on the Mount. It was perhaps the most decisive speech uttered by a follower of Christ up to that time, for it was a major surgical operation. It cut the Christian movement free from Jewish grave clothes and said, "Loose it and let it go"—let it go to be a universal redemptive movement. Up to that time it was in danger of being absorbed as a Jewish sect, but now Stephen's decisive words cut the Jewish bondages and the Christian movement was free; it was on its own under God. But it cost the life of Stephen, the first martyr, to do it.

Perhaps that is symbolical: The layman must now cut the cords that bind the Christian faith to an official priestly class and universalize it once again. They must give it back to the people, the people of God, the laity.

The church at Antioch was founded by laymen, carried on by

laymen, and spread through that ancient world by laymen. It was a lay church. That is important for the reconstruction of the church of today; the next great spiritual awakening is going to come through the laity. Hitherto, the center of gravity has been on the minister, now the center of gravity has to be shifted to the laity. We ministers, missionaries, and evangelists are never going to win the world. We are too few to do it and if we could do it it wouldn't be good, for it would take away from the laity that spiritual growth and development which comes through sharing one's faith.

But we will never get the laity to take the responsibility for the Christian movement and its spread by saying: "Come on and help the pastor." Their inner response, and sometimes outer response, is: "Why should we? That's his job. We pay him for that." If we are really to get the layman, wholeheartedly get him, he must see and feel his own standing and responsibility in the Christian movement. So both Protestants and Catholics have begun to interpret that standing and responsibility of the laity in the Christian faith and movement. Two books have come out, one by Dr. Kraemer, a Protestant, entitled *A Theology of the Laity,* and another by a Roman Catholic, *Toward a Theology of the Laity.* A Roman Catholic, hearing me speak on the laity, said: "I'm surprised, for all we hear now in our churches is 'laity.' " Hitherto, it had been the hierarchy of the priests. A significant change. And greater changes are ahead.

For we are discovering that the Christian movement was and is a lay movement. Jesus was a layman. The Jewish leaders asked Jesus for his credentials: "By what authority do you do these things?" He had none, had none except the changed people around him: "The blind receive their sight, the lame walk, the lepers are cleansed, the dead are raised, and the poor have the Gospel preached to them." His credentials were the transformed people around him. And then he added this: "And blessed is he who finds no occasion of stumbling in me." That is interesting and penetrating; for it would ordinarily be: "Blessed am I if you find no occasion of stumbling in me." But he put it the other way: "Blessed are you if you find no occasion of stumbling in me—and my credentials." For those credentials are not from "authorities," but from the authority of the facts produced, changed lives. They, and they alone, are the only valid religious authority of the future. "By their fruits shall you know them."

Moreover, the apostles were laymen. There is no record that any hands were laid on them in ordination. They were ordained: "You have not chosen me, but I have chosen you, and ordained you" (John 15:16). The choice was the ordination. So if there is a line of "apostolic succession" through the laying on of hands, the apostles were not in it.

Then the apostles began to act as if they possessed the movement instead of the movement possessing them. They argued over who was "first" in the movement, wanted to call down fire on the Samaritans who refused to receive them, forbade people to cast out devils because "they followed not us." So Jesus had to re-lay the lay character of the movement. He did it in appointing the seventy laymen. "After these things (the things I have mentioned: quarreling over first place, calling down fire, forbidding others to cast out devils) he appointed seventy others," sent them out two by two, and gave them the same commission he gave the apostles, namely, that he was immediately behind them, that those who received them received him. They came back jubilant: "The devils are subject to us in thy name." (The apostles couldn't get the devils out of a boy, because the boy had a better case of devil-possession than the apostles had of God-possession.) "In that hour Jesus rejoiced: 'I thank thee, Father, that thou hast hid these things from the wise and prudent, and hast revealed them unto babes.' " "The wise and prudent" were the apostles and "the babes" were these untrained laymen. New power had been tapped for the movement, lay power.

A crisis arose, as reported in Acts 6 over the distribution of food; the race issue lifted its head. The Greeks claimed their widows were neglected in the daily ministration. The apostles did a wise thing: they appointed the Seven and placed them over the food distribution; all of these had Greek names. But they did something else not so wise: "They said it is not befitting that we should forsake the word of God and serve tables. We will give ourselves to prayer and to the ministry of the word." And they appointed others to look after the material side. This seemed wise and spiritual, but actually it was unwise and unspiritual. They drove a wedge into life between the material and the spiritual. They separated what God had put together in the Incarnation. In the Incarnation the Word was made flesh, the spiritual was to function in material terms; they were two sides of one reality. The Christian faith was to function in material terms. But they put the spiritual apart and above, unrelated, and put the material lower, unredeemed. That division is still with us today and it is a disastrous division. It has produced the very problem we are wrestling with now—the irrelevance of the Christian movement in not being related to life. The root reason for that charge of irrelevance is this division between the spiritual and the material. They are two sides of one reality. If the spiritual does not function in material terms it does not function.

What happened? A strange and unexpected thing: the center of spiritual power shifted from the Twelve to the Seven, shifted to the group that held life together, spiritual and material. It was Stephen, head of the Seven, the lay group, who precipitated the revival in Jerusalem, which won "many priests to the faith" and brought on his own martyrdom. It was Philip, another member of the Seven, who first preached the Gospel outside Judea, went to Samaria, and all Samaria turned to the Lord. It was Philip again who first preached the Gospel to an Ethiopian and, through him, helped to found the Ethiopian church, still extant. It was Philip who had "four unmarried daughters who prophesied." Prophecy there was not the foretelling of events, but the forth-telling of the Good News, the beginning of the ministry of women. This was the beginning of Christian spinsterhood—unmarried daughters; an ancient and honorable order of women who marry themselves to human need, and who have been very fruitful around the world. (Incidentally, I paid tribute in one of our Ashrams to the Christian spinsters, especially on the mission field, for what they had contributed to human welfare. The spinsters met the next day and made me an "Honorary Member of the Ancient Order of Christian Spinsters"—a title I've worn proudly!)

Then Paul took over, in large measure, direction of the Christian movement. He says, "I went up to Jerusalem and those in authority gave me nothing." He got his grace and apostleship directly from God. Harnack, the church historian, says that "all the early conquests of Christianity were carried out by informal missionaries." Everyone who received the Gospel gave the Gospel. So the Christian faith spread clear over into India and up into China through the Nestorians—"a church on fire."

This went on till the third century when at the Council of Nicaea a change took place: laymen were pushed to the edges, and the clergy, especially the bishops, took over the Christian movement. It has continued thus until today. To be a layman after Nicaea was "a concession to human frailty"; they were second-class citizens in the Kingdom of God. Today in the Franciscan Orders they belong to the Third Order with the Priests as the First Order and the Nuns as the Second. I have talked to the Franciscan Third Order and found them intelligent and very responsive, but they are third-class citizens of the Kingdom of God, according to the system.

The laity, on the whole, have been in the stands as spectators, and the clergy have been on the field playing the game. If the clergyman kicks a goal or makes a touchdown he is applauded: "Good pastor, hope he will stay." That setup must be changed;

the laity must come out of the stands as spectators and take the field as players; and the clergymen must come off the field as players and take the sidelines as coaches of a team. The clergymen must be the guides, stimulators, and spiritualizers of an essentially lay movement. Downgrading them? No, upgrading them. For it is greater to be a coach than to be a player. It is better to get ten men to work then to do ten men's work. As guide of an essentially lay movement the pastor's work will be vitalized. Their audiences will look up to them on Sunday morning and inwardly say: "Pastor, we have taken on ourselves jobs too big for us and our resources. Introduce us to resources which will make us adequate." That would vitalize listening and vitalize preaching, vitalize the whole service, the whole church. The church would be a filling station and a checkup station for a long and hard week's run for the laity.

This putting together of the material and the spiritual is illustrated by an Indian judge who presided at a function set up for me in Kerala, South India. While a judge he used to spend an hour in private devotions between four and five o'clock each day and then, still kneeling, he would write the judgments of the day. A Brahmin lawyer got out of hand one day in his court. The judge said: "I'm sorry, but I'll have to fine you for contempt of court." The lawyer replied: "Your Honor, if you fine me I will take it as the very judgment of God. For when you speak, God speaks." He took divine justice and turned it into human justice—the sacred into the secular—they were one!

The Chief Justice of Rhodesia, Sir Robert Tredgold, resigned when the new constitution was put through by the white minority, saying: "I cannot administer a constitution so unjust to the African majority. My Christian conscience will not allow me." A layman was far ahead of the church which, for the most part, was silent and acquiescent, acquiescent to a basic wrong.

When C. T. Venugopal was an M.A. Brahmin student in Madras, he accepted Christ in one of my meetings. He went home that night on a tramcar and, as he reports it, "Jesus sat alongside me on that tramcar and I knew that we belonged to each other forever." When he became a member of the Railway Board in charge of the finances of the government-owned railways of India he took divine love and turned it into the solution of bitter human relationships. His Brahmin private secretary heard me tell of the reaction of two American clergymen when they heard Dr. Kagawa speak: "Well, he didn't say much, did he?" And the other replied: "When you are hanging on the cross you don't have to say much." This Brahmin secretary said to me: "When you told of Dr. Kagawa it reminded me of Mr. Venugopal. He, too, is hanging on the cross and he, too, doesn't have to say much." He did not merely put the cross as a slogan in the midst of secular life, he put it there with himself on it. That made a difference, one would be the Word of the Cross become word, but this made the Word of the Cross become flesh.

A leather worker, a chamar, a very low caste, had lost his son by death. A missionary sympathized with him and ended by saying: "Remember, God is love." The chamar's face lighted up and he replied: "Yes, I know God is love. No one could work for Foy Sahib without knowing that God is love." Here was an Englishman in colonial days, where the atmosphere said, "God is Law," saying by his life and attitudes: "God is Love," the Word of love become flesh in secular situations.

Solly McCreless came forward in one of my meetings in college, came forward to get a call to the ministry. Instead, he got a call away from the preaching ministry into the ministry of serving God through business. He showed me where on the streets of San Antonio, Texas, a friend loaned him five hundred dollars to get started in the insurance business. Now he has as an expression of his Christian faith an insurance business, American Life and Hospital Insurance, with several hundred million dollar assets and directed toward Kingdom ends. "Your call into the serving ministry through business was just as valid and just as vital as my call into the preaching ministry," I said to him.

"What is the basis of your business?" I asked Mr. Comer of the Avondale Mills. His answer: "First, we give a basic wage equal to any union wage. Second, we set aside 5 percent for the investors. Third, we go fifty-fifty for the rest of the profits between the business and labor over and above wages. Fourth, we bring in labor and make some of its members a part of management." "Any conflicts?" "No, we are a family." "Profits?" "We are eighth in the national economy." It is a cooperative order in the midst of a competitive one, an example of loving your neighbor as you love yourself.

At the close of a service club meeting in London, Ontario, Canada, the leading industrialist came up to me and said:

You're right. My factory was a feud. I was giving as little as possible and my men were doing as little as possible. So we were tied in knots and getting nowhere fast. I called in the men and said to them, "We are both on a pagan basis of 'Thou shalt love thyself,' Let's change it to a Christian basis, 'Thou shalt love thy neighbor as thyself'. Hitherto, I've had the right of hiring and firing in my hands, now I put it into yours. You decide who comes into the factory and who stays in. And we will set aside 23 1/3 percent of the profits for labor above wages. We will work it out together." My factory turned from a feud to a family overnight. I didn't have to weed out slackers; labor weeded them out, for they were now slacking not only against capital, but against labor as well. It was to everybody's interest to work and to work hard, for the more everybody worked the more everybody received.

A cooperative order worked well for capital and labor.

But if capital hesitates about a cooperative order in industry, so does labor. I put up a labor-capital management proposal before a Chamber of Commerce meeting, proposing a labor-capital management and a division of the profits and losses between capital and labor. A labor union organizer came up to me at the close and said: "What are you trying to do? Are you trying to put the labor unions out of business?" I saw in a flash that both capital and labor were organized on the basis of competition with each other, a dog-eat-dog economy instead of a brother-help-brother economy. Both of them need to be converted from the pagan basis, "Thou shalt love thyself," to a Christian basis, "Thou shalt love thy neighbor as thyself." It would be for the benefit of both, in spirit and in production.

If someone suggests that this is the word of a Christian evangelist, then may I suggest the word of an official of the First National Bank of Chicago after an address to the parent Rotary Club: "We were very interested in what you said in Rotary today about profit sharing. You may be interested to know that when we as a bank take over a business to finance it, the first thing we try to do is to get the business to put in profit sharing. We don't do it for charity, but through sound business procedures. It makes for better relationships within the business and more production." The Christian way is The Way, the way to run a business.

In the reconstruction of the church, let the laymen of all churches organize themselves into an "Organization of Christian Employers and Employees to put Christian Principles into Industry." They could be the demonstration centers of Christianity in the secular world and the leaven for a new order. There is a field for the witness of laymen where it counts. Then instead of *Culture Against Man,* written so penetratingly by Jules Henry, we would have a *Culture for Man.* The culture and the basic Christian convictions would coincide not conflict—cooperation in convictions and cooperation in culture. That would resolve a basic strain in modern secular life. It would also allow Christianity to be true to itself without a basic compromise. Christianity and Christians could both be at home in a society that is basically Christian, loving your neighbor as you love yourself.

This can be accomplished by laymen demonstrating the new order. It will not be accomplished by the clergy preaching at the old order to change into the new order. That would be the word of the new order become word. The demonstration by lay-men would be the word of the new order become flesh. We need both, but the major emphasis must be not on the demand, but on the demonstration.

The reconstruction of the church must be by laymen who are in a position of being at the core of secular life, and thus can change it from within by demonstration of the new order at the base.

Conclusion Number One: The church of the future must be primarily a lay church, with the laymen as participants playing the game; and with the clergy on the sidelines as the coaches of a team, as the guides and spiritualizers of an essentially lay move-ment.

III

A SOCIETY OF THE CARING

The next element in the Antiochan church which can be embodied in the reconstruction of the modern church is the element of caring—the Antiochan church was a church that cared. When a severe famine fell upon Jerusalem and the rest of that ancient world, the church at Antioch "agreed to make" a contribution, each according to his means, for the relief of their fellow Christians at Jerusalem. This was an important moment in the life of that nascent church. Suppose that church had passed a resolution of sympathy and assurances of prayer and had sent it to Jerusalem, it would have possibly fixed the attitude for future reactions to economic problems. It would have been the word become word—a word of sympathy and a word of prayer. Christianity would have been manifested as idealism and not as realism.

But fortunately their reaction was realism. "Each according to his means" meant it was not an ordinary collection, but a collection that was thoroughgoing and one that set a standard. Giving in the Christian faith was to be "according to one's means"—the greater the means, the greater the responsibility, not merely as a principle but as a practice. And as a practice not indefinitely postponed, but immediately carried out: "So the disciples agreed to make a contribution, each according to his means. . . . This they did." They did not pass a resolution and then "pass the buck," but their agreement became an action immediately carried out. They did not appoint a committee to get the facts and report back to a future meeting, a subtle way of avoiding responsibility by postponement. It was not a debating society—it was a deciding society. It was "a society of the caring" and a society of the caring to the point of sharing. The caring became a sharing—not an emotion, but a deed.

That was important. It brought out clearly that the only thing you believe in is the thing you believe in enough to practice. Your creed is your deed. Your creed is not something you point to in a hymnbook and repeat on Sunday morning. It is something you decide upon every day of the week and every hour of the day. It is a working principle, or it is a worthless principle.

Two important principles emerge—here was a church in which the creed and the deed were one and the agreement to decide and the decision to do were one. That is the characteristic of the lay mind at its best. The clergy dealing as it does with ideas often put a hiatus between the creed and the deed, and another hiatus between deciding to do and the actual doing. There are exceptions, of course. But the rule has been so obviously the hiatus that when we think of the church today we think of debate rather than doing, of dialogue rather than decision. The fact that the modern church could switch so readily from evangelism as decision to evangelism as dialogue or discussion, and do it without any searching of heart, showed the prevailing church climate. The church is at home in dialogue, it is not at home in decision. When I asked Dr. Altizer if he had helped anybody with his "God is dead" movement, his reply was: "I am not a counseling pastor, I am a theologian." Theologians are not supposed to help people to decide higher issues—they are supposed to discuss and debate abstractions about God and life!

When someone asked a YMCA higher official what was the secret of the success of the YMCA movement, he replied: "I suppose the secret is this: We see a need; we pray about it; we go out and do something about it." The usual church climate is: "We see a need; we pray about it; we discuss it." Not always, for there are glorious exceptions, but that is the prevailing climate in the churches. Therefore, we open the churches once a week to have a religious service instead of having them open seven days a week for service to the community.

So we say that the next great spiritual awakening is to come through the laity and one of the characteristics of that revival would be the creation of a climate in the churches where the churches will see a need, pray about it, and then go out and do something about it. For the lay mind at its best is pragmatic and decisive—it has to be in modern business if it gets anywhere. We need the breath of that spirit in the reconstructed church, where much of its life is "sicklied over" with unrelated or irrelevant thought.

But to return to the fact that the church at Antioch responded to the need of the famine-stricken Christians at Jerusalem apparently without solicitation. The account reads: "a severe famine . . . (which occurred in the reign of Claudius) ." "So the disciples put aside money . . . for a contribution"—that word *so* is revealing. "A famine occurred. . . . So—." Without exhortation, without begging, without oratory they responded to a need because they were sensitized. They were "a society of the caring." Baron Von Hugel, a Roman Catholic layman, gave this penetrating definition of a Christian: "A Christian is one who cares." This group "cared," not only spiritually, but economically as well. They made no distinction between a spiritual need and a physical one—it was human need and as such they responded to that need. The Christian faith responded to that need whether it was physical, spiritual, mental, or social. It responded to need. Jesus taught people, healed people, and fed people all as a part of the coming of the Kingdom of God. He didn't say, "Now I'll heal you and feed you if you come and follow me." The healing and feeding were not bait to get them to follow him. The healing and feeding stood in their own right—they were answering human needs, and Jesus came to meet total human need. So the Christians were sensitized to human need, in anybody, anywhere. That is important, for "life is sensitivity." The lowest life is sensitive only to itself. The higher in the scale of existence you come, the wider the range of sensitivity and the deeper the depth. When you come to the highest life ever lived on this planet, the life of Jesus, you find complete sensitivity: "I was hungry and you fed me; in prison and you came unto me; sick and you visited me; a stranger and you took me in." When the righteous asked, "When?" he replied: "Inasmuch as you have done it unto the least of these, you have done it unto me." He was hungry in their hunger, bound in their imprisonment, lonely in their being strangers. One thing he left out: "I am sinful in your sin"—that would have been misunderstood, but at the cross he became just that. He was crucified between two thieves as one of them, and he cried the cry of dereliction which we have to cry when we sin: "My God, my God, why hast thou forsaken me?" He became sin for us. Here was complete sensitivity, therefore complete life, for "life is sensitivity." You can tell how high you have risen in the scale of life by asking one question: "How widely do I care, and how deeply?" Someone has put it this way: "The extent of the elevation of an animal and of course, any rational being, can be infallibly measured by the degree to which sacrificial love for others controls that being." Some are sensitized to themselves—they live in a state of self-reference—they are low down in the scale of existence. Others are sensitized to their family—they live in a state of family reference—a little higher, but not much. Others are sensitized to their class or their race, but some are sensitized to persons, even enemies.

To be Christianized is to be sensitized. I mentioned previously a blind man who sat alongside the road begging when Jesus passed by. He called out to Jesus: "Have mercy on me." The disciples told him to shut up. They had no interest in blind beggars. Then Jesus turned and said, "Bring him to me." Then the disciples rushed to the man and said: "Arise, he is calling you." They were not interested in the blind beggar until Jesus was. They followed Jesus' interest. They were sensitized by his sensitivity. That has been happening ever since. Humanity is becoming more and more interested in his interests. In Jesus' day the pious Jew every day thanked God that he was "not born a leper, a woman, or a Gentile." When Jesus announced his program in the little synagogue at Nazareth, he let the people know how far he was going with his program of liberation: "There were many lepers in Israel but to none was the prophet sent but to a Gentile, a Syrian, Naaman. There were many widows in Israel but to none was the prophet sent but to a widow of Zaraphath." What was he saying? That God cared for lepers, women, and Gentiles especially! He was quietly but decisively cancelling their daily prayers! The people of Nazareth were furious. They took him to the brow of the hill on which their city was built to cast him down headlong. They would have nothing of his sensitivity. But he glanced this way and that, they fell back, and "he passing through the midst of them went his way"—his way, not theirs. Since then the world is following more and more "his way"—not theirs. The world is more and more filled with institutions and movements to lift the depressed classes of the world. And now nations have taken up the movements which he alone started and which his followers almost alone carried on through the ages. Now "to each according to his need" is being silently adopted in national programs. Partly from Christian principles and impulses and partly from fear of Russia. The fear of Russia, if not "the fear of the Lord," is the beginning of social wisdom. But from one motive or another the needs of men everywhere are more and more on the consciences of the world. But "to each according to his need" is straight out of the New Testament practice inspired by the presence of the living Christ. And sooner or later this principle will be followed by the operation of another Christian principle: "From each according to his ability"—"If a man will not work, neither shall he eat." The operation of that principle is more difficult than the first, for you can give to people according to their need out of superficial sympathy and pity; but to inspire people to give back to society according to their ability after their needs are met is to produce character which will not eternally cry, "Give me," but will be developed enough to say, "I give to you." It takes more Christian sensitivity to make contributive men than to give contributions to men. But both are needed. And Christ produces both. He produces men who see need and want to meet need, and he also produces men who want to produce men who see need and want to meet that need. The Creator produces creators who produce creators. The end of creation is creation.

All this is based on a God who cares. The God we see in the face of Jesus Christ is a God who cares—cares enough to give himself on a cross. That is the ultimate in caring. After I had spoken to a large predominantly Hindu crowd, a Hindu doctor, the chairman, arose and said: "We must not involve God in the affairs of this world. He is lifted above all these things. We must not humanize God." In other words, to him God was a God who did not care. But a God who doesn't care doesn't count. The God who would sit in awful isolation from eternity contemplating his own perfection would be a God who would be the center of cosmic misery. For the law of happiness in this universe seems to be: Center yourself on yourself, and you won't like yourself. Lose yourself in the needs of others, and you will find yourself—find yourself a happy person. That is the basic law of life, human and divine, in this universe. Break it and you get broken—there are no exceptions.

In *Culture Against Man*, Jules Henry in his analysis of Chris Lambert describes him as one who fits a stereotype of adolescence.

Remote from his parents although he does not hold them in "utter contempt," hating dependence of any kind, so that he looks on any human association as threatening; distrustful and contemptuous of others as well as of himself, he makes grandiose identifications which cause him to be even less self-confident and to feel he is wasting his life (for he is not yet approaching the stature of Leonardo, Newton, or Joyce). He feels lonely and isolated because he is distrustful and fears involvement; and he fears his involvement because he is distrustful and because involvement requires some accommodation to others. It is better to let things happen to him than to make them happen. Already the fear of being just like everybody else and hence dying to his Self ("I'll be just another person") casts its shadow on his future.[1]

That is the picture of young and old, of God and man, of everybody who doesn't care, who does not want to be involved with others and their problems and troubles. So he becomes inextricably involved with himself and his own problems and troubles. "I couldn't care less," he says as a life characteristic, so now he has to care more—distressingly more—about himself. He is the payoff.

So the church of tomorrow will be the society that cares—today. The people who will rule tomorrow are the people who care today. But it must not be a limited caring—it must be a caring beyond self, family, class, race, and creed. It must be care universal—even for enemies. I write this seated in a building built by the Dutch in 1744, now an Indian Government Rest House, overlooking a beautiful harbor, Cochin. There have been a succession of rulers—Maharajas, Dutch, Portuguese, British, Congress, and now Communists. Each has been superseded because it cared for itself rather than for the interests of the people. The Communists promised most for the people, and were put in power a few years ago, but were superceded by the Central Government because they used the

---

[1] (New York: Random House, 1961), pp. 258-59.

machinery of government for Communist Party purposes—they cared for themselves. So they were put out of power. An appointee of the Central Government ruled. Then a Congress Government ruled, and they were put out because they fought among themselves—two types of Congress Parties. Now the Communists are back in power because they made greater promises of caring for the people. Now the period of disillusionment is setting in. They are slipping back into a limited caring—caring for the Communist Party instead of the common people. The situation is crying out for a political party of the unlimited caring. The world situation is crying out for a society of the unlimited caring. This is the basic world need.

The church could be and is, by its very structure, destined to be the answer to that world need. For it has within its structure two things which could be the program and the power for that society of the universal caring. The two things are: the Kingdom of God—the program; and the person of Jesus—the illustration of, and the empowering for, the society of the universal caring. No other society has this built-in structure, which by its very nature makes caring easy and makes it imperative. It is the one society that is structured for caring. If it doesn't care it violates its own nature. In a Brahmin society the God behind it is noncaring, and if you care it is in spite of the noncaring background; you care not on account of God, but in spite of God. In a strictly competitive culture, if you care you do so in spite of the culture. In a Marxian Communistic society, you care with a limited caring—you care for Communists. Toward the non-Communists the attitude is described by Mao: "We work, not with love, but with a hammer." But if you sow a hammer you will reap a hammer. If you sow antagonism you will reap antagonism. So it is no mere chance that the hammer and the sickle go together in that order: sow a hammer and you reap a hammer; the sickle is the symbol of reaping. So communism while initially successful, goes to pieces on the rock of limited caring. It doesn't love its enemies, it liquidates them, if possible.

Only the Christian society by its very nature provides the background of a caring God and a caring Redeemer who both love their enemies. They overcome evil with good, hate by love, and the world by a cross. That produces the society of the caring.

But this society of the caring has to exist in the midst of a society which at its basis says, "Care for yourself." Now note: the Christian society of mutual caring does not say "Love your neighbor," but it does say "Love your neighbor as you love yourself." Your self is included in your caring. There are three basic urges in human nature—the self urge, the sex urge, and the herd urge. The self urge is obviously self-regarding, the herd urge is other-regarding, but the sex urge is partly self-regarding and partly other-regarding. So there are just two urges in human nature—the self-regarding and the other-regarding. The Christian faith says: "Thou shalt love thy neighbor" (the other-regarding urge) "as thyself" (the self-regarding urge). It exactly balances the caring; you are to care for others as you care for yourself, and you are to care for yourself as you care for others. This saves the caring from being an overbalanced caring for others and a neglect of one's self, or an overbalanced caring for oneself and a neglect of caring for others. In both cases the unbalanced virtue becomes a vice. It must be a balanced virtue or it is not a virtue. And yet we are trying on a world scale to organize life around individualism—the self-regarding urge—as in "the free nations," or around collectivism—the other-regarding urge, as in "the Communist bloc." And further, we are preparing to fight it out in a ruinous world war to decide which half-truth will prevail. All the time sanity is standing over against this insanity with the offer of the Kingdom of God, where both of these urges are put together in a living blend—"loving your neighbor (the other-regarding) as you love yourself" (the self-regarding). The conflict would be over and the Kingdom of God on earth would begin.

It is the destiny of the reconstructed church to put into operation this kind of caring. If we can do this, then we have come to the Kingdom for such a time as this. For nothing is so absolutely necessary as this kind of a caring on a world scale.

In the meantime we are wasting our time and loyalties and emotions on unbalanced, limited caring. On the one hand, the book *Care for Yourself Only* is gaining a following among youth by the insistence on the necessity and duty to care for yourself alone. This will result in a crop of disillusioned middle-aged people and old people who will be self-centered, cynical, insistent on having their own way and then not liking their way after they get it, and on expressing themselves and then not liking the self they express. For it can be said as a proved dictum: Every self-centered person is an unhappy person—no exceptions. For every self-centered person is in violation of his own nature—the other-regarding urge is unfulfilled and in rebellious unhappiness.

On the other hand, the collectivists are out to impose their collectivism by force of arms. I write this in Allepey, India, where long lines of laborers march with uplifted, clenched fists, chanting "Inquilab Zindabad"—"Long live revolution." They would impose "Love thy neighbor" by force. The means automatically cancel the ends. You cannot use wrong means to get to right ends. For the means preexist in and determine the ends. Wrong means lead to wrong ends—automatically. So Marxist communism will break itself upon two rocks— the rock of a limited caring (they care for Communists only, the rest are liquidated) and the rock of the use of wrong means leading inevitably to wrong ends.

Between these two extremes we have various types of limited caring—those who care for their families only, then those who are sensitized to their class only. For instance, two British ladies stood in a shop in Naini Tal, India, when it was raining as only it can in the monsoon and one said, "Look at that poor sergeant out there. He is getting soaked." The other replied in disdain,

"But he is only a sergeant." Had he been a commissioned officer he would have gotten terribly wet! She could feel class pain but not human pain. She gave me her number—"I have not been sensitized except to my class. I've only risen slightly in the scale of existence. I'm partially developed." Then there are those who are sensitized only to their race. The race riots in America are saying to the world: "America is only a partly developed people—they are sensitized to their respective races, but not to persons as persons." Of course, there are millions who in America are sensitized to a person as a person. They are the saving salt of our democratic and Christian civilization. But even some in the churches are not yet Christianized in this regard.

But when the churches are truly Christianized and our civilization is truly civilized, then our country will be "the society of the caring." In the meantime the reconstructed church-must be the society of the caring, and thus be the Word of Caring become flesh. For the wave of the future is in the direction of a society of the caring. The future belongs to the caring—to those who care most widely, most deeply, and most sincerely. The church of Jesus Christ is destined by its very makeup and calling to be that society of the caring.

Nothing is more needed in society than this sense of mutual concern. For the culture in education, in business, and in society is competitive—jostling for recognition, for money, and for power. It is largely pagan, modified slightly by the Christian ethic and spirit. The whole pressure is pagan—"thou shalt love thyself." But society, education, and business won't work unless they work in the Christian way—"Thou shalt love thy neighbor as thyself." So the Christian society of the caring is the hope of our society; and without it we decay and perish. The reconstructed church, as it becomes deliberately and of set purpose the society of the caring, is destined to save society if it can be saved. Apparently it is our only hope.

In a round table conference, when I asked, "What is your biggest headache?" an Indian Christian lawyer replied: "My biggest headache is to see the general deterioration of morals permeating all society." That is the headache of society, East and West, a headache to those who see, and to those who participate in, and are a part of, that deterioration. It is the world's headache. All other headaches are marginal. This headache is central and all-pervasive—except in a Christian society of the caring. There life is attuned to the laws of the Kingdom of the caring, and hence, no inward clashing and no headaches. I asked an employee of the Income Tax Department of the government here in India: "What is your greatest headache?" For of all the centers of headaches this department would presumably be the very center, for it is generally said that business concerns in India have three sets of books—one for the proprietor, another for the partner, and a third for the government! The Christian income tax officer replied: "Headaches? I don't have headaches—I'm a Christian." Dr. MacLaughlin, of the Woman's Medical College of Philadelphia, a psychiatrist, says that 99 percent of all headaches are rooted in the mental and spiritual. So the headacheless person is a person who knows how to live. He is adjusted to God, to himself, to his fellowmen, and to life. He is the Christian. A society of such people would be the society of the caring. That society of the caring would be so busy caring for the cares of others that they would have none of their own. Legend says that the way birds got wings was this: They took weights on their wingless shoulders and those weights turned to wings. That is not legend—that is life. The weights we take on our shoulders for others become wings for ourselves. The society of the caring would be the society of the soaring. Like the lark, as they soared they would sing. But like the lark they would have their nests in the sod—in the sodden places of the earth, that sodden lives might share their soaring and their songs.

Now when I mention the sod and the soaring this brings together the material and the spiritual which in the church at Antioch were parts of one whole. They cared for the physical needs as a part of their spiritual caring. Life was one. The division of life between the material and the spiritual is a false division. In the Christian faith they are one. Unless the spiritual functions in material terms it doesn't function. The housewife who put a cardboard sign up over her kitchen sink, "Divine Service Here Three Times a Day," had the right relationship with the material—washing dishes was "Divine Service." Feeding the hungry was feeding the hungry—and Christ; serving others was serving him. So a society of the caring for physical needs only is a half-caring. A society of the caring for spiritual needs only is also a half-caring. The society of the caring is a society of the caring—fullstop, no qualifications. Anything that concerns man concerns them. So the Kingdom is a total Kingdom with a total caring. A partial Kingdom with a partial caring is self-defeating. "If you love only those who love you what reward can you expect? Surely the tax gatherers do as much as that." A reduced caring is a cancelled caring. The world is suffering from a cancelled caring: Communists caring for Communists, a competitive society caring for a competitive society, race caring for race, class for class, denomination for denomination, party for party. Nowhere do we find the unlimited caring. Nowhere except in one place, the Christian movement when it is truly Christian. Some Quakers were feeding people at the close of the last world war. A Polish woman asked them, "You feed everybody?" "Yes." "Poles?" "Yes." "Germans?" "Yes." "Russians?" "Yes." "Jews?" "Yes." "Atheists?" "Yes." The woman drew a deep sigh and said, "I knew there ought to be people like that in the world but I didn't know there were."

Now note: "I knew there ought to be people like that"—that "ought" from the lips and heart of a Polish woman going through the aftermath of a cruel and devastating war is really the summed-up cry of humanity everywhere: "There ought to be people like that in the world." For without people like that, individual and collective life is a torture instead of a triumph, a hades instead of a heaven. That "ought" is not merely the sigh

of a suffering woman. It is the commonsense demand of a world stumbling from crisis to crisis, not knowing how to live. For life in its inner structure is made to be lived in this way of mutual caring and if we try to make it work in some other way it breaks down. So this "ought" is not only a call—it is a destiny. We "must" live in this way or not live at all. So we are being "called" and we are being "pushed" into the fulfillment of a destiny—the destiny of the society of the universal caring. A Christian is one that cares and a Christian society is one that cares universally and illustrates it in the particular, in "the particular" in which it operates or ought to operate. It must be the Word of Caring become flesh.

Conclusion Number Two: The church of the future must be the society of the caring, particular and universal caring.

IV

A CHURCH THAT HOLDS
TOGETHER DIFFERENCES

In the church at Antioch there were "prophets and teachers." The teacher is usually the conservative, gathering up the values and lessons of the past and passing them on through the next generation. Teachers are an important factor in society. They may be professional teachers, or they may be amateur teachers—teaching by their example and precept the values which have been valuable in the experience of society. Without the conservative, society is like a mariner starting on a voyage without chart or compass or star to steer by. He has to inch his way into the future by fresh experimentation every moment, a confused man.

A professor, talking to a brash young man, when asked what he was doing, said that he was a professor of history. He saw by the young man's face that he wasn't impressed or interested. The professor asked him: "Aren't you interested in history?" "Nah," he replied, "I believe in letting bygones be bygones." His "nah" revealed his mentality—he was living by a "nah," a no, a negation, and he was a negation. The person who does not learn from the past knows nothing in the present and will know nothing of the future. He is a rootless being and therefore a fruitless being. He who does not stand on the shoulders of the

past to view the present and the future is like a babe crawling amid his toys learning life by touch.

The conservative is a necessary element in human society. Without him we start blank. But without the radical, life stops with the past and we lack progress. The prophet is usually the radical, wanting to apply values to wider ranges of life. He strives to break the molds of the past and strives to give the privileges of the few to the many.

In any society both of these, the conservative and the radical, are necessary. If we were all conservative we would dry up, and if we were all radical we would bust up. But between the backward pull of the conservative and the forward pull of the radical we make progress in a middle direction. A French philosopher has said that "no man is strong unless he hears within his character antithesis strongly marked." So if a man is only conservative he is weak, and if he is only radical he is also weak. But the conservatively radical and the radically conservative are strong.

The Christian faith is both radical and conservative by its very nature. The center of the Christian faith is a person. Jesus was conservative and Jesus was radical. He sums his attitude up in this sentence: "I came not to destroy but to fulfill." This is the most radically conservative and conservatively radical utterance ever uttered. "I came not to destroy"; those who come to destroy are pugnacious, negative, and eventually militaristic. They destroy, with any weapons, at any cost, and without discrimination, the good wrapped up in the thing to be destroyed, as well as the bad. The difficulty with that attitude and method is that like produces like. Destruction produces destruction. The destructive method produces destructive reactions which destroy the destroyer. "Those that take the sword shall perish with the sword." The dust heaps of the centuries are mute witness to that fact uttered by Jesus. Every destructive nation or civilization has been destroyed and will be destroyed. So Jesus, announcing the most radical conception and program ever presented to the mind of man—the Kingdom of God—disassociated himself from the destructive—"I came not to destroy."

That renunciation of the destructive made him the most constructive person and his program the most constructive program ever presented to humanity. Here is where he outlives the Communists. In the temptations in the wilderness Jesus confronted three alternative ways to bring in the Kingdom. He had just been baptized "when all the people were baptized." He had stepped into that line of repenting people as they came to be baptized "unto repentance" in John's baptism. He who needed no repentance took a baptism of repentance and identified with us at our lowest point. He would save people from within, by identification even with their sins. "He became sin for us." There was a reaction—is this the way to bring in the Kingdom? For forty days in the wilderness he meditated and prayed and struggled with alternatives. Then the Tempter suggested three: "You are the Son of God, that is sufficient. Don't go back as you began. Feed yourself apart; make these stones into bread. Live aloof on miracles. The multitudes will then come to you." The temptation of the ascetic. India has fallen into that temptation—to her impoverishment. So much so that she has now set up a department of government to rehabilitate the "sadhus," the ascetics of India. The second: "If you must go back, don't go back as you began. Don't stand with the people in their sin as one of them. Stand on the pinnacle of the Temple, be looked up to and worshiped and bowed down to. Be the symbol of religion, lifted up and looked up to. If you do go down to the people, cast yourself down, and God will put you back on your pedestal by miracle, special protection of your prestige and power." Jesus rejected both.

The third, "If you do go back, I'll show you how to get the kingdoms of the world. Bow down and worship me, take my methods. The only thing the people understand and will respond to is force. Use it to bring in your Kingdom." Jesus rejected that. He would use his own method to get to his own ends. And that method was simple—love, self-giving love. The Communists have fallen into this third temptation: Any means are right that get you to your ends of communism, including force and force especially.

If Jesus rejected these three methods what method did he choose? He chose the simplest and profoundest method ever presented: "I came not to destroy, but to fulfill." "But to fulfill"—that is the most revolutionary and the most constructive method ever proposed and acted on. He would destroy a wrong system by fulfilling any good in that system and incorporating it in the new and presenting something so much better that the old wrongs in that system would drop away like an outworn shell. The good kernel in the old had been assimilated in the new; it was fulfilled and destroyed by the very fulfillment. It was lost in a higher life. Jesus did that with the law. He did not destroy the law. He rescued out of the mass of ordinances and rules and regulations two commandments, "Thou shalt love the Lord thy God," and "Thou shalt love thy neighbor as thyself," and made them the center of his Kingdom. The law as a law dropped away, fulfilled and superseded.

We can fulfill communism by receiving out of the heart of the system two principles: "To each according to his need" and "from each according to his ability." These two principles make the system float, weighted down as it is by materialistic atheism and an impossible morality ("Anything is right that gets you to your goal.") , and by its tyranny and world aggression. But these two principles are embedded in the Christian faith. Distribution was made "according to each one's necessities"; and "if a man will not work neither shall he eat"—distribution according to need and contribution according to ability. These two things came out of the Christian Scriptures. Suppose we would accept those principles as our own and set them to work in our free society, what would happen to communism? It would fall off as a dead leaf.

Take another realm. A Hindu member of the Indian

Legislative Assembly, chairman of one of my public meetings, said: "Thirty years ago, when I was a student in Forman Christian College I heard Stanley Jones and I still remember the title of his address: 'Karma and the Cross.' For weeks we discussed that address inside the classroom, and outside, both professors and students." Why? I had put my finger on the nerve center of two great systems: karma is the nerve center of Hinduism, and the cross is the nerve center of Christianity. They seem destined for head-on collision: In karma you reap what you sow, there is no forgiveness; in the cross we reap forgiveness by the act of God. When I showed that others reap what we sow, it opened the door to the vicarious, the door to our reaping what Christ sowed in sowing himself on the hill of Calvary. If there were one at the center of life as God and man, could he pass on to every member of the human race the result of his sowing? Could we reap his karma and not our own if we surrendered to him and identified ourself with him? That's possible. Did it happen? Well, if it didn't happen, it ought to have happened. For men will die for men and pass on to them the karma of their sowing themselves. Will God do that? "Would I suffer for one I love? So wouldst Thou, so wilt Thou."

By recognizing the truth in karma that we reap what we sow, and by fulfilling it by showing that we can reap what God sows on a cross, we fulfill it and destroy it at the same time. The whole system of karma as an individual sowing and an individual reaping and the whole system of transmigration go down with that fulfillment for it is superfluous and unnecessary. We can be saved by grace instead of being punished or rewarded by transmigration. These corollaries drop off like a dead leaf—made irrelevant by fulfillment.

Take another: The basic conflict between capital and labor is over whether labor will be treated as hired hands, or as an integral part of the business. If the former, then the basis is conflict, with labor trying to get as much as possible and capital trying to give as little as possible. If the latter, the basis is cooperation, manifested in a labor-capital management and a division of the profits and losses; in other words, a cooperative order between capital and labor. This is conservative. It conserves the truth and the driving force in both capital and labor. Under this cooperative order, capital would probably get less spectacular monopolistic profits. The profits would be cut down for capital when shared between capital and labor. But it would be more even, for strikes and lockouts would be eliminated, and they are very expensive and ruinous to both. In the end the profits would amount to more and be more dependable for both. For in sharing profits labor would have an incentive to produce more, for the more they would work, the more they would produce; the more they would produce, the more they would receive. Now labor has no such incentive. The more labor works, the more someone else receives—the owners. That lack of incentive for labor is the sand in the industrial machine. If capital and labor would agree to a labor-capital management and a division of the profits and losses, it would "fulfill" both capital and labor and result in the destruction of the labor-capital conflict by the emergence of a cooperative order.

Take another. I write this in the city of Calcutta where idolatry of the crassest kind is rife. The commandment, "Thou shalt not make any graven image," has not cured the world of idolatry. For the commandment lives on by the truth in it—it brings "God" near and approachable. That truth must be fulfilled before idolatry can be destroyed. In Jesus that truth of God being near and approachable is fulfilled. "Jesus puts a face on God," brings God near, and makes him approachable. Jesus is the human life of God—God approachable, God lovable, God simplified. Jesus represents God in a human environment, in human terms. And when I say "represents" I mean represents. If you want to know what God is like, look at Jesus. He is "the express image of God." God is a Christlike God. But idolatry misrepresents God. When Jesus said, "He that hath seen me hath seen the Father," we can believe that gladly. But when the idol says in substance, "He that hath seen me hath seen God," we doubt it—gratefully doubt it. For if God is like the idols we see, then God is unworthy, irrelevant; wooden or stony, and sometimes crooked in character. I said to a priest in a temple: "Do these frescoes of the gods in their lewd acts help you when you come to worship." The priest replied: "You have to be morally strong when you come to this temple, otherwise you will go away and do what the gods do."

So Jesus fulfills what idolatry brings—the necessity of a God that is near and approachable. Jesus is "Emmanuel, God with us." He fulfills the necessity of having God with us, but in the fulfillment he destroys idolatry. For we see that Jesus represents God and idolatry misrepresents God. So the fulfillment fulfills the good and destroys the evil. This is conservative and radical.

Jesus puts together the radical and the conservative in these words: "The Kingdom of heaven is like unto a householder who brings forth from his treasure both the new and the old." "The new" is the radical and "the old" is the conservative, and we need both. For something happened in history—Jesus Christ—that needs conserving. If we lose Jesus Christ we will lose God and everything that Jesus brought, and that is *all*. A Unitarian came up to me after a service and said: "Can't you come to one of our Unitarian conferences and help us to get God back into Unitarianism. For we are losing God and becoming a humanism." I thought to myself: "This is interesting. I, who have emphasized Jesus Christ, have found him and I have found God. The more I know of Jesus, the more I know of God, and the more I experience Jesus, the more I experience God." But here is a movement that specializes on God and bypasses Jesus, and that has lost both God and Jesus, and is becoming a humanism! So the Christian faith is conservative—it conserves the most precious gift of history, Jesus Christ. For it brings forth "the old." But it also brings forth "the new"—it is radical. It undertakes to apply the principles and spirit of Jesus to the whole of life, individual and collective. It undertakes to do nothing less than replace the present unworkable world order with the Kingdom of God on earth, the most radical proposal ever presented to the mind and will of man. So the new is first—"new and old." The Christian faith while deeply conservative leans toward the radical. But it is profoundly both.

So the reconstructed Christian church after the pattern at Antioch would hold in a living blend both the conservative and the radical in a living fellowship. Now these two groups have drawn apart; the conservatives in one camp and the radicals in another, to the impoverishment of both. They need to cross-fertilize each other, and produce a Christian faith that is radically conservative and conservatively radical.

Forgive this personal reference but it is apropos: A conservative journal printed an article, titled, "Is Stanley Jones a Modernist?" which came to the conclusion that "he has a fundamental soul and a modern mind"—a blend I would like to illustrate. So far as I am concerned the controversy between fundamental and liberal is destroyed, for in Jesus the good of each is fulfilled. The rest drops away.

Conclusion Number Three: Suppose there were a reconstructed church which would hold within itself the conservative and the radical in a living blend; and further suppose that church would hold within itself the living principle: "I came not to destroy but to fulfill"—fulfilling every good found everywhere and by that very act destroying the evil around that good; and suppose that church should help others in society to do the same, as individuals and groups. Would not that church be indispensable in the future? The answer, Yes!

V

HOLDING TOGETHER
A CLASSLESS SOCIETY

If the reconstructed Christian church is to be a blend of the conservative and the radical, it must also be a society beyond class. In the church at Antioch was a true classless society. In that society, as a teacher or prophet, were "Simeon, called Niger," literally the Latin word meaning "black," from which we get the word Negro, a man probably from Africa, and Manaen of "the court of Herod." One was probably low-class socially and the other probably high-class. But these two men representing low and high social classes were in a society where there was no consciousness of any difference in class. They were both sons of God, one in the family of God, equal before God, and therefore equal before men. Class was gone!

The Christian society, when true to itself, is a society of the sons and daughters of God, a family of God. The statement of Jesus is this: "One is your Father" and "all ye are brethren"—a family of God. In a family there is no class. So this does not reduce us to the class of the proletariat, it raises us to the family of God. Every person is "a person for whom Christ died." We are all equal before God, therefore equal before men. This gives us an equality upward. It makes a man put back his shoulders and respect himself. "Why don't you accept your inferiority?" asked a Brahmin of a Christian of low caste origin.

"How can I?" answered the Christian, "for I'm literally not inferior. I'm a man for whom Christ died." "What has your Christianity done for you?" asked a Brahmin policeman of an outcaste Christian. "For one thing I'm no longer afraid of you," replied the Christian.

And this is not mere boasting; it is the recognition of a positive fact. Jesus' attitude toward the underprivileged is based not on sentimentality, but upon sense. We have been following the interest of Jesus in the underpriviliged and find we are following sense. The interests of the Son of Man are increasingly the interests of the sons of men. Take every interest Jesus had and every one is becoming increasingly the interests of humanity.

He was primarily interested in the Kingdom of God; it was the center of his message: a new total order that would replace the present world order with a higher order, God's order, the Kingdom of God. And this was to be on earth: "May thy Kingdom come . . . on earth." The rise of modern totalitarianisms can be directly or indirectly traced to his emphasis on the Kingdom of God. Said some German leaders after I had spoken on the Kingdom of God: "You seem to sense why we turned to Naziism. Life was compartmentalized and at loose ends; we needed something to bring life into total meaning and goal. We turned to the wrong totalitarianism—Naziism; it let us down in blood and ruin. We now see that what we were seeking for was the Kingdom of God." Whether expressed or unexpressed, that will be, and is, the inmost thought of the still existing totalitarianists as they see their systems creak and groan on their way to dissolution. Their deepest prayer, uttered or unuttered, is: "May thy Kingdom come . . . on earth." Their true interests are following His interests, but they don't know it.

Take another interest. Jesus said, "One is your Father." The idea of the one creative God who stands in relationship of Father and Sustainer is more and more becoming the collective interest of humanity. If there is a God, then he ought to be the

God that Jesus revealed in his own character and teaching. If he is like Jesus Christ in character he is a good God and trustable. We could ask nothing higher, and we could be content with nothing less.

A corollary: If God is our Father, then men are our brothers. "One is your Father" and "all ye are brethren." The oneness of humanity under the oneness of God is an ultimate view of humanity and God. And is the evidence of the discovery of science bearing this out? Yes. If anything is emerging about humanity it is this: There are no permanently inferior races and no permanently superior races. Given the same stimulus and the same incentive the brain of humanity will come out about the same. A headmistress said this to me recently: "We have all classes and all castes in our school. The first few years those from the outcastes are slightly inferior in the examinations. But by the time they arrive at the level of the high school the outcastes have shed the inferiorities imposed by society and the examinations show no difference between them and the higher castes." The student who stood at the top in Calcutta University, where there are tens of thousands of students, was from the headhunters of Assam. There are infinite possibilities in everybody, everywhere. So when Jesus took nobodies and made them into somebodies—took fishermen and made them the teachers of the world and entrusted them with the most precious teaching ever entrusted to the human race—he was in the wave of the future. The future is following him in its interests in the underdeveloped peoples of the earth.

Take the interest Jesus had in little children. His disciples rebuked the mothers who brought the children to him, but his reply has become a classic in regard to children—has influenced the attitude of the world toward children more than anything ever uttered: "Suffer the little children to come to me and forbid them not, for of such is the Kingdom of God." Here he focused the attention of the world upon the most important member of the human race—the child. Philosophers, statesmen, empire builders had passed by the child as insignificant. Only Jesus said: "Suffer the little children to come unto me." And for a very good reason: "For of such is the Kingdom of God." Their attitudes toward life, their simple receptivity, and their position in life as the most important members of society, those who will make up the future society, make children the focus of attention. But until Jesus called little children to him the attention of society was elsewhere and otherwise. The vivid symbol of change is found in the Fiji Islands, where a stone, on which the skulls of children were once crushed, is now a baptismal font where children are baptized. "As the twig is bent, so the tree will grow" is the favorite maxim of educators and psychologists, and people in general focus their attention upon the child. "Jesus set the child in the midst"—the midst of whom? Everybody. And he said: "He that hurts the soul, the body, the mind of a little child, it is better that a millstone be tied about his neck and he be drowned in the midst of the sea." If the child is "in the midst" of attention today it is because Jesus, an unmarried man, set him there!

Take another interest of Jesus: the home. A homeless man with nowhere to lay his head defended one institution, the home, founded it on one man and one woman, true to each other till death parted them. Death parted them—spiritual death, adultery, or physical death. Death alone should part them. Where that conception and practice are held, the home is stable, the participants are happy, if not *on account of,* then *in spite of.* But where this conception of the home has departed, the home is unstable and the participants disrupted and the children delinquent. Ninety-five percent of juvenile delinquency comes out of broken homes. The Chinese say: "In a broken nest there are no whole eggs." So modern society, flouting Jesus with one hand, is pulling away its own foundations with the other. Society will have to come back to the conception of Jesus—or perish. So perforce the attention of society is drawn to the home and we must follow his attention—or perish.

Take another simple statement: "Put up your sword; they that take the sword shall perish with the sword." Around that statement have been more discussions, more debates, more national conferences, more personal and corporate concern then any other statement in human history. The United Nations is built up to implement this statement, teaching how to disarm, how to get rid of war. The world tension we are in is all due to our collective disregard of this statement of Jesus. A lone man makes a statement which upsets a world and makes a world frantically try to obey it: "Put up your sword." Moreover, the last part of that statement has been fulfilled in history: "They that take the sword shall perish with the sword." The dustheaps of the centuries are mute witnesses to the fact that every military nation has perished with the sword. So we are perforce compelled to follow the attention and interest of Jesus.

Concerning another interest, Jesus said: "He that saveth his life shall lose it, and he that loseth his life shall find it." Center yourself on yourself and be a self-centered person and your self will disintegrate, and you will lose what you try to save. But if you lose yourself in the service of others, your life will come back to you, happy, adjusted, creative. Jesus repeated that sentence five times. Psychologists and sociologists and clergymen have repeated it five million times and more, for life is saying it and saying it with repeated emphasis.

Take another even more universal truth. When Jesus was asked, "What is the greatest commandment in the law?" it was a crucial moment in the history of humanity. For suppose he picked out the wrong commendment, we would all go wrong with him. There were thirty-six hundred commandments in that law. It would be easy to pick out a marginal or irrelevant commandment, as, for instance, the Sikhs have done in picking out five signs of being a Sikh: Long hair, a comb, a bracelet, everworn drawers, and a dagger. Not one has any relevance to human living. They missed relevancy in all five signs. Suppose Jesus had done the same in picking one. It would have relegated him to the limbo of the forgotten. But he went straight to this one: "Thou shalt love"—love God and love man. He put his finger on the supreme value in human living—love. Was he right? The search for that supreme value in human values has gone on for centuries. The result? Dr. Smiley Blanton, a psychiatrist, wrote the book *Love or Perish*. He meant just that—love, or you perish, perish here and now. The inner cohesions break down and you go to pieces as a person. You perish. But another psychiatrist, perhaps the greatest of America, came to the conclusion that the patients in the sanatorium under his control were there not because they did not know what was the matter with them (the basis on which psychiatry had worked), but because they hadn't loved or been loved. So they decided they would make all their contacts love contacts—they would love their patients into loving. They tried it for six months and when they took stock they found that the average period of hospitalization was cut in half. The patients were getting through in half the time. Then they knew what the basis of the patients' sickness was—they were not loving or being loved. But that discovery was of the utmost importance, for Jesus had said two thousand years ago that the supreme value in human character was love—"Thou shalt love" God and man. And psychiatry comes along two thousand years later and says, "Thou shalt love"—or "you're sick and you will never be well until you do love." Psychiatry has had to follow the interest of Jesus or become sterile itself.

Take another principle: "He that would be greatest among you shall be the servant of all." That is the most quietly revolutionary principle ever uttered. Men of all climes and all ages have attempted to be great. Jesus asked, "Who by taking thought can add a cubit to his stature?" Well, men have taken thought in attempting to add a cubit to their stature, to make themselves great. They have piled up possessions around themselves, but the possessions have possessed them, and choked them to death; they have piled up titles after their names (I saw a Maharajah with six lines of titles after his name, a name I have forgotten!) ; a general piled up a pyramid of skulls to "add a cubit to his stature" but his name is forgotten, his memory overshadowed by the dark shadow of the pyramid of skulls; monuments have been provided to perpetuate names—we see the monuments and forget the provider. When France voted for the greatest Frenchman, they chose Pasteur and bypassed Napoleon. Why? Because Pasteur served the people and Napoleon served Napoleon. Pasteur fulfilled the idea of greatness as announced by Jesus: "the servant of all shall be the greatest of all." Napoleon made the many serve him and his ambitions; Pasteur served the many. Humanity in rendering its verdict follows the interest of Jesus and discards the opposite. Many democracies call their ruler the Prime Minister, the First Servant. And when they are convinced that he is no longer the First Servant of the people but is serving himself instead, they will vote him out. He can't be "First" unless he is "Servant." And it has to be "servant *of all.*" If he serves "some," himself, his party, his favorites, then he is breaking the law—"the servant of all"—then the law breaks him and out he goes!

Take something else that has been rejected by the builders of civilization but is becoming the head of the corner: "The meek shall inherit the earth." This has been looked down on by the proud, the vaunting, the self-assertive as a slave mentality. But it is now more and more looked on as the way, the only way, to inherit the earth—be meek! The proud, the know-it-all, know nothing. The great scientists are the meek—they follow the facts wherever the facts lead them, or they wouldn't be scientists. So the meek inherit the earth—they inherit it, for they are meek enough to surrender to the laws and facts of nature, thus learning nature's secrets and how to harness those secrets to the development of the earth and to the development of men. The proud, know-it-all mentality is eliminated. Only the meek, the receptive, inherit the earth. This verse sums up the attitude and the result: "How blest are they who know they are poor;

the kingdom of heaven is theirs" (Matt. 5:3 NEB). If they are poor enough to receive, then all the resources of the Kingdom of heaven belong to them. They belong to the Kingdom of heaven, but more amazing still, the Kingdom of heaven belongs to them; all its resources are at their disposal, provided they are poor enough to receive, provided they belong to the meek who inherit the earth and the Kingdom of heaven as well—everything on earth and heaven belong to those who are meek enough to receive them.

But why labor the obvious. The obvious is that every single thing Jesus was interested in and everything he insisted upon is now becoming and will increasingly become the interest of humanity; that is, if humanity is to survive.

Jesus was not a moralist imposing a set of morals upon humanity for which humanity is badly made. Rather he was a revealer of the nature of reality, lifting up the laws underlying the universe. He seldom used the imperative, almost never the subjunctive, almost entirely the indicative. He kept saying, "This is, and you must come to terms with it." When he finished the Sermon on the Mount "the people were astonished at his teaching, for he taught them as one having authority." As one having authority is literally *exousia*, "according to the nature of things." So what he was speaking of was not imposed but rather exposed, exposed out of the nature of things. Hence it is realism, not idealism.

To sum up this section of our study of Antioch, we find that the search for principles and for people is more and more following the interests of Jesus. Jesus lifted up principles and he lifted up people, and humanity today is more and more following him in its interest in the same principles and in the same people; or humanity is decaying to the degree that they depart from them. That result works with an almost mathematical precision. Those who follow Jesus' interest in principles and peoples, although they may not name his name, go up; if they reject them, they go down. There is something at the heart of the universe which is working for Christ and with Christ: those who align themselves to that something are in alignment with the redemptive purposes of the universe, and they go up in proportion to that alignment or they go down as they depart from it.

The Son of man is for the sons of men, and anything that stands against their rise must go down before the fact of his judging, redeeming Presence. The status seekers who seek for status lose both the status and the seeking—it all ends in disillusionment and disappointment. They break themselves upon the law of the Kingdom: *He that would be great among you shall become the servant of all.* There is, and there can be, no other way to greatness except to greatly serve. And the catch is in that word "all." Some are willing to be servants of some—my family, my class, my race, my nation. It is a road to a dead end. The cynical disillusionment of this age is a direct result of breaking that law.

If the church—the reconstructed church—blindly joins the status seekers by jostling for status by costly buildings or expensive equipment, it will also end in disillusionment. There is one and only one way to gain status and that is to be the servant of all. But if you serve all just to gain status, that, too, will end in disillusionment, for in the end you are not serving "all,"—you are serving yourself through the outward serving of all. Down deep it is the ego seeking greatness by pretending to serve all.

The weakness in the law of karma is in the motive of service. A Hindu social worker said the difference between the Hindu motive for social service and the Christian is this: "We serve for something, you serve for someone." Meaning: "We serve for something—for our store of good karma, which in turn will turn out to be a better birth in a future life. But the Christian when he is truly Christian serves for someone—for Christ. But it doesn't end in serving someone—we also serve the someones. "Inasmuch as you have done it unto the least of these you have done it unto me"—the religious and the humanitarian motive become one. That is important; if we make our motive solely for him then "we screw ourselves up so high we are of no use for anything beneath the sky." But if we do it only "for someone," then the humanitarian motive grows thin and the humanitarians grow cynical and disillusioned. You can't believe long in man unless you believe in something more than man; something that gives man worth and value in spite of his capacity to blunder and to sin. The solely religious people aspire and sit on spires, and the solely humanitarian perspire and tire. But the Christian knows that when he is serving someone—"one of the least of these"—he is doing it unto him. He is doing it *for* "someone" and *to* "someone"—the motive is the same.

A Hindu, head of a Hindu social service organization, said to me: "Our social workers lack motive. Could we send our workers to work in your hospitals and schools for a period to learn and catch your motive?" If they did, they would run straight into the person of Christ and into the principle: "Inasmuch as you do it unto one of the least of these, you do it unto me." If you lose Christ you lose the humanitarian, and if you lose the humanitarian you lose Christ. For the principle works both ways. "Inasmuch as you did it not unto the least of these you did it not unto me." This negative portion, which is seldom used, is important, for it means that you cannot have the religious unless you have the humanitarian—they are one!

This principle of doing social service for something, or doing it for some One and someone is the dividing line in motives. It may prove the decisive dividing line. Those who serve for some One and someone will outlast and outwear those who serve for something, for personal advantage, a cause, a party, or a state. This "some-thing" motive wears thin and grows weary as the thing to which it is attached is attractive or tarnished in the wear and tear of human experiment. But doing social service for some One and someone has a wearing quality in it that will outlast the pagans who do it for something.

So the reconstructed church must be a society of one class—the class of those "for whom Christ died." If it is other than that it is other than Christian.

I was about to speak in a large public meeting in Hartford, Connecticut, in which the setup was interesting: three men were assigned the task of interpreting the needs of that large audience. One, a businessman, told of the needs of the businessman; a clergyman told of the needs of the clergy; and finally a youth told of the needs of youth. "Now," said the chairman, "you have heard of the needs of this audience, please speak to those needs." I arose and said: "I'm interested in your method of running this meeting and appreciate it. But you interpreted the needs of this audience and left out labor, and you left it out unconsciously. That shows where the Christian movement is set in society, the upper-middle classes, but it is unconscious of the needs of labor. And yet Jesus, the center of our movement, was a carpenter. Are we to turn over labor to the Communists for guidance?" It was a quiet Judgment Day, a Judgment Day needed.

That same quiet Judgment Day becomes vocal in the burning buildings and the looting mobs that issue out of the ghettoes of America, crying the same "Inquilab Zindabad," "Long live revolution." We may disagree with this manifestation of the revolution, especially as one of them said publicly: "I like sitting in a second-story window and taking potshots at Cadillacs as they go by." But the church must be the center and the guiding spirit of this revolution and guide it into an economy closer to the beginnings of its own movement where distribution was made "according to each one's needs." Down underneath is the leaven that is leavening society. It is the basis of the world ferment, it has its roots and origin in the Christian faith, and it should be carried on by that faith. Equality of opportunity is the birthright of every man born in a democratic society. And since democracy is the offspring of Christianity, then the church—the reconstructed church—should produce that classless society inherent in itself.

So this item in the reconstructed church must be one of high priority, namely, a Christian church must be a classless society, where every person is looked on as a child of God and therefore is of infinite worth, where every person is a person "for whom Christ died," and therefore is of infinite worth; and more, every person is a person of infinite possibilities through that redemption.

Conclusion Number Four: The reconstructed church must be a society where this passage is fulfilled and brought to embodiment: In Jesus Christ there cannot be Greek or Jew (race distinction), *barbarian, or Scythian* (cultural distinction); *bond or free* (social and economic distinction); *circumcision or uncircumcision* (religious distinction); *or male or female* (sex distinction). (See Col. 3:11 and Gal. 3:28.) *We are all equal before God and must be equal before man. The new church must be beyond class.*

VI

THE CHURCH AND RACE

What has Antioch to teach us about race? Its teaching is important and it is incisive—and needed. And it is uncomplicated, with no patronage, no restricted acceptance, and no so-far-and-no-farther. It is simple and straightforward, with no weasel words.

It took a miracle and a voice from heaven (the descending sheet) to cure the race prejudices of Peter. Even then he went to the Gentiles at the house of Cornelius patronizingly: "I need not tell you that a Jew is forbidden by his religion to visit or associate with a man of another race."

But now look at Antioch and breathe this breath of fresh air: "There were at Antioch in the congregation there certain prophets and teachers: Barnabas, Simeon called Niger . . ." (Acts 13:1). Simeon, the black, was a prophet or a teacher in the church at Antioch. Among others he laid his hands on Barnabas and Paul to send them forth to preach the gospel to white Europe and hence to white America. We are Christians because a Negro laid his hands on Paul and Barnabas to preach the Gospel to our white ancestors, hence to us. For without that Negro's hands on Paul and Barnabas it would not have been a Christian commission—it would have been less than Christian and other than Christian.

I was about to speak to 10,000 people in the auditorium in Kansas City, Missouri, on Reformation Sunday. To me, it was coming on a pilgrimage to a shrine. For in that auditorium in 1928 at the General Conference of the Methodist Church, I was elected a bishop one night, and I resigned the next night after a tortured day of indecision. When I resigned my joy was back, my call secure: I was to be a missionary and an evangelist to America and the world, to all men everywhere. I was inwardly excited in getting back to this Holy Shrine to kneel at the altar of a dedication.

But imagine the slap in the face I received as I entered the auditorium and saw a man walking up and down carrying a placard with these words on it: "Can you give me a quotation from the New Testament teaching integration?" Apparently no one had given him any such quotation for he was still walking up and down assuredly displaying his banner, and had been doing it for some time previously. So before I gave my address I publicly read this passage: "There were at Antioch, in the congregation there, certain prophets and teachers: Barnabas, Simeon, called Niger."

Suppose this "Christian" brother had been right and suppose there had been no such passage. What would have happened to our Christian faith? It would have been jammed into a racial pot labeled white and there it would have died—pot-bound. It couldn't be universal for what is not universal is not true. Two and two make four is universal, the same everywhere, for everybody. Two and two make five is local—by its very nature it cannot be universal. So in trying to keep the Christian "white," this man was trying to make it less than universal and therefore less than true: it was false. He was attempting to kill the very faith he held.

Moreover, if he had been right, and there was no such passage, and no such attitude in the Christian faith, then he would have canceled my call to be an evangelist to all men everywhere. Moreover, the auditorium which was to me a shrine of dedication would have become a Wailing Wall, where I would have been compeled to stand and bewail the fact that I had nothing whatever to give to the majority of the human race, the colored races of the world.

For mind you, the period when we could go paternally to the colored races and say in reality: "I've come to pick you up with tongs, but I can't touch you, nor can you touch me,"—that is gone and gone forever. Thank heaven. We must go with a Gospel of equal standing, equal respect, equal opportunity, and equal worth, or we do not go at all.

So the woman who said: "Everything is being integrated but, thank God, we still have our churches left," was wrong. She didn't have "our churches" left, she had a mausoleum of dead attitudes which she called "our churches." Christ had departed, leaving them dead. For you can't shut out any son of man without shutting out the Son of man.

If the reconstructed church attempts to compromise on the race issue and incorporate exclusive white spots in it, they will be "white spots" of leprosy and consequently "white spots" of fear. For the walls that divide man from man and nation from nation are falling, and will continue to fall. For science and the Christian faith are converging on this conclusion: there are no permanently inferior races and no permanently superior races; there are only developed and underdeveloped races. Given the same stimulus and the same incentive the brain of humanity will come out about the same.

But Christianity came to that conclusion first, came to it naturally and spontaneously. That phrase "certain prophets and teachers: Barnabas, Simeon, called Niger," is an explosive and revolutionary phrase. There is enough dynamite in it to blow our existing social order to pieces. But—and this is the point —it was put in without comment and with no sense of surprise as if something extraordinary had happened. It slipped in as if it belonged there, it was the native air of Antiochan Christianity. It belonged. Now after two thousand years of wandering in the wilderness of racialism we return to where we began and think we are doing something strange and revolutionary. No, this is not strange and not extraordinary; it is natural and normal, because it is Christian.

Science is coming to the same conclusion, but more slowly, by the method of experimentation, the method of following the facts. It is verifying, and will more and more verify in the future, that humanity is one.

This year I made a pilgrimage to a spot which will be a shrine in the future because it is a landmark in the upward march of man. The outcastes of Kerela were the lowest of India. If a Brahmin walked along a road and met an outcaste the outcaste would have to step off the road and let the Brahmin pass at a certain distance lest he pollute him. The roads to the temples were denied him lest he pollute the temple. These outcastes, awakened by the Gandhian movement, adopted the method of nonviolent noncooperation and sat alongside the road for a year and a half in torrential rain and blistering sunshine. They would be sent to jail as trespassers, but would come out and sit down again. And India has a tremendous capacity to sit! If you don't pay your debts, your creditor will sit on your doorstep until you do. Those patient outcastes fighting a lone battle for freedom were joined by Brahmins who were touched by them. After a year and a half the road was thrown open. And more amazing still: all the temples of India were thrown open to them. And more amazing still, a member of the outcaste community, Dr. Ambedkar, piloted the new Constitution of a free India through Parliament, and more amazing still: wrote the Bill of Rights under which Brahmin India has now to live. That Bill of Rights makes it a criminal offense, punishable by fine or imprisonment, to discriminate against anyone, in any situation, because of his caste.

Now note the distance those outcastes have traveled—lone sitters on a temple road in silent protest: road thrown open, temples thrown open, and the gates of opportunity thrown open by one of their number. Dr. Ambedkar, because he was the ablest constitutional lawyer in India, did it out of sheer ability.

There are no permanently inferior peoples; everyone has infinite possibilities. America will be a richer and freer country when everyone in America stands equal before the law, stands with equal opportunity to rise, socially and culturally, economically and politically, morally and spiritually.

The church of the future must show the way. In Antioch there were not two churches, one white and the other black. They were one. A little white boy of eight sat alongside a Negro Bible teacher at lunch in one of our Ashrams and said to him: "I liked everything you said today but one thing I could not understand. You kept saying, 'My people, my people.' Why do you say 'My people'? I thought we were one people." That boy was right. We must not have two Americas—one white, the other black. We are, and must be, "one people." Nor must we have two churches, one white and the other black. We are "one people," devoted to one Lord and belonging to one kingdom and one brotherhood.

I was in Rhodesia and saw with dismay that white Rhodesia was following in the footsteps of South Africa in trying to make the Africans subordinate and inferior. Then I heard this: In Old Umtali, which is in Rhodesia, thirty young Africans, twenty-four male and six female, took the Cambridge University examinations in a foreign language and 100 percent passed, some of them with honors and at the top of the thirty was a girl. These papers were marked in Britain. I said to a friend: "That marks the doom of apartheid in Rhodesia. You cannot keep down people like that."

I know the diehards will die hard and protestingly. But the future belongs to man, not to man as white or black. The segregationists will only segregate themselves. I wrote of the outcastes having to get off the road when a Brahmin passed. But the tables have turned. Some depressed class Christians were having a procession in Kerela. They met a Brahmin on the road, and though there was water on both sides of the road, the Christians, now conscious of their dignity and rights, stayed on the road. The Brahmin, to avoid them, had to get out into the water up to his neck and let them pass. He was shaking with impotent anger but was helpless. If he still wanted segregation—he got it! Up to his neck in it!

The roads—all roads, economic, social, political, and spiritual—now increasingly belong to man as man, not to man as Brahmin or outcaste, black or white. This applies to the churches, and to the churches especially, otherwise we will find ourselves up to our necks in our own self-imposed segregation.

The lovely thing about giving up segregation and giving equal opportunity to all is that when we do it, we are back home. For that is where we began and that is our native land. We have been in an alien land of racialism, now we will be at home in the Kingdom.

Conclusion Number Five: The reconstructed church must be "a house of prayer for all nations," and all races and colors; or else it will be "a den of thieves" where we steal privileges intended for all and try to make them exclusively our own. But if they don't belong to all, they belong to none. For if not shared with all, they disintegrate, they rot.

VII

STRONG MEN DIFFER— AND HOLD TOGETHER

In the reconstructed church there must be a basis so strong that strong men can and do hold together in spite of differences. For this necessity will arise in every church, especially in a church in a democracy where opinions are freely expressed and freely decided upon. This necessity arose in Antioch. In Jerusalem where the apostles were in charge the point at issue would have been referred to the hierarchy, a decision given, and the case closed, or a split would have taken place if a sufficient minority were involved and sufficiently strong men were leading it.

But there was no such hierarchy at Antioch. They had to come to a common agreement among themselves or there was no agreement. How did they hold together? It was very simple and very effective; they held together around the person of Jesus Christ. They were Christ-ians.

Suppose they had been drawn together around some other center—this doctrine, that doctrine, a mode of baptism, the bishopric, or this or that type of bishop, this gift or that, this person or that—what would have happened? Confusion and division. No human thing, no human custom, no human person can hold any religious movement together for long. Only divine shoulders can bear that responsibility, only a divine person, lifted up, "will draw all men" to him.

This verse is decisive: "He that gathers not with me scatters." If this means anything it means that if we gather around Jesus, if "Jesus is Lord," we can transcend all our other differences and find a unity in a common Lord; but if we don't do that, if we gather around something else, however good, we scatter. Christcentric we gather; any-thing-else-centric, we scatter.

Strong men, Barnabas and Paul, at Antioch were illustrations of this principle. After they had returned to Antioch from their evangelistic tour in Asia and Europe, Paul felt the call of the beyond upon him and said to Barnabas: "Let's go back and see those whom we have led to Christ in our last tour." "Good," said Barnabas, "and let's take John Mark with us." The face of Paul hardened, "No, we can't take a man who turned back at Pamphylia on our last tour. We must have a pure movement." "Yes," replied Barnabas, "but remember we must have a redemptive movement. We don't break a man when he makes a break. We preach the Gospel of the second chance, the third chance. The Christian movement is a redemptive movement." "Yes," replied Paul, "but first of all it is a pure movement." Now these were two perfectly good ideas that could have been organized into two perfectly good new denominations, around two perfectly good men: "The Barnabasites, or the redemptionists," and "the Paulites, or the purists."

But while they parted "in irritation" with Barnabas taking John Mark and Paul taking Silas, they were "commended to the grace of God" by the church, as much as to say, "Brothers, you both need that grace." Nevertheless, they came back to Antioch, it was their home. And they were still one in spite of their differences about John Mark, for they were *Christ*-ians, one in Christ. They differed about John Mark—they were dedicated to Christ. So they held together in him.

The reconstructed church must be centered in Christ. If so, then strong men and women can afford to differ about John

Mark issues, for the Christian faith is not founded upon John Mark but upon Jesus Christ. Here our simple formula of the Ashrams is to the point: "If you belong to Christ and I belong to Christ, we belong to each other."

As someone has put it: "Be entirely committed to Christ, as for the rest be entirely uncommitted." If you are entirely committed to Christ, then you can afford to be yielding in other things where there is no great principle involved. That is what Paul meant when he said: "Let your yieldedness be known unto all men" (Phil. 4:5, Wesley). Does that mean that we are to be wishy-washy, agreeing with everybody, in everything? Hardly. Paul was silken at the edges, but steel at the center. "Circumcision availeth nothing, nor uncircumcision, but a new creature." A rite was nothing, but being right in life was everything. But if a person is insistent that he is right about everything, big and little, then he is wrong about everything. For one who is always right is always wrong, wrong in his very attitude of being always right. Paul was right in saying John Mark should not have turned back at Pamphylia and wrong in insisting that he should not be given another chance.

There is one place and only one place where you are always right—at the place of Christ and when you are showing his spirit while at that place. There you can let your full weight down.

Someone has said: "By the grace of God it is well to learn that you may be mistaken." Paul was mistaken—about John Mark. He was right—about Christ. About John Mark he had to hunt for arguments to bolster his position; about Jesus the arguments bolstered Paul. He could not let his full weight down on John Mark, on Jesus he could. So a church built on John Mark issues is argumentative—it has to be; built on Christ it is assured—it doesn't have to argue, it witnesses.

I picked up my morning paper not long ago and a paragraph said:

With major decisions still to be made on appropriations for defense, Vietnam, the poverty war, foreign aid, model cities and other programs, and with gun control and the nomination of Abe Fortas to be chief justice still to be fought over, members of both House and Senate took time out for sometimes bitter political debate.

The whole machinery of government of a great nation stalled while the marginal issues of political parties occupied the center. The marginal occupied the center.

I look across the aisle of this plane where I am writing and a nice-looking youth with long hair and a beard kept stroking his mustache, his beard, and the long hair—kept on doing it after he fell off to sleep, the subconscious taking over when the conscious abdicated. The marginal, the attempt to be different, occupied his waking and his sleeping hours, occupied him and made him a marginal-issues man instead of a central-issues man, sidelined him. He wasn't in the game of purposeful living.

One young person said of her family: "In our family we major in the minors." If the church majors in the minors, it will be a minor issue in society—sidelined.

We are in a crisis in history, a big one. In a similar crisis when the Communists were taking over Russia, a large convocation of the Orthodox Church was debating whether to have a certain color of priestly garment in a certain place in the church ritual. Debating that when the color of Russia was turning—Red!

The reconstructed church of today must be streamlined to the central and fundamental issues of life, life for today and forever. Take a fine-tooth comb and comb the account of the church at Antioch and you cannot find one single thing that was marginal, trivial, or not worthwhile. Everything that happened in Antioch had destiny in it. What happened there is vital and relevant for us today. In fact, we are in our churches today and are adherents of the Christian faith today because Antioch listened to God and exhibited a type of Christianity which was truly Christian, therefore truly relevant and world changing. Cut out Antioch and you cut out the heart of the Christian expansion in the world. You would have to rewrite the history of the world and rewrite it with the greatest and most beneficent impact that ever touched it left out.

This is a fluid period of human history. Christopher Fry puts it in these vivid lines:

> Dead and cold we may be, but this
> Is no winter now. The frozen miseries of centuries
> Cracks, breaks, begins to move.
> The thunder is the thunder of floes,
> The thaw, the flood, the upstart spring.
> Thank God, our time is now when wrong
> Comes out to face us everywhere
> Never to leave us till we take
> The longest stride of soul men ever took,
> Affairs are now soul size.[1]

Affairs are now soul size, for the future is in them—they are big with destiny. Now the bad is really bad, for it presages a bad present and a bad future; and the trivial and the marginal are also bad, for they occupy the place of the good and the vital and the relevant.

When Paul wrote, the majority of mankind were termed "the uncircumcised" by the Jews: "You went in to the uncircumcised and ate with them." The term was central with the Jews. Paul put it on the margin where it belonged; more, he put it beyond the margin as irrelevant. "Neither circumcision availeth anything or uncircumcision, but a new creature." In other words, religious rite, or its absence, is irrelevant; the thing that matters is a new creature, a transformed person. Translated into the vernacular of today this would mean: "Neither candles

[1] From the play *A Sleep of Prisoners*. Reprinted by permission of Oxford University Press.

availeth anything, nor uncandles; apostolic succession nor nonapostolic succession; rite nor its absence; tongues nor non-tongues; secularism nor nonsecularism—none of these, none except a new creature." Everything must be brought to the bar of one judgment: does it produce a new creature both in the individual and the corporate life? If so, it stays; if not, out it goes. We must be stripped for action, Christian action, the action that produces the new creature, individually and collectively.

John Mark may be good or bad, but if he divides the Christian faith and the Christian movement, he is bad. He and everything like him belong to the margin; Christ belongs to the center, for he is the center. If the Christian faith or the Christian movement gets off that center, it is ec-centric—off center and therefore out of power and redemption. It is a wire cut off from the dynamo; light cut off from the sun; a river cut off from its source; life cut off from Life—Christianity cut off from Christ, hence unchristian.

When Marco Polo visited Kublai Khan, the great Mongol chieftain, the latter sent an urgent message to the Pope, requesting him "to send to the Mongols a hundred Christian teachers well learned in the seven arts and well able to prove that the way of Christ is best." Marco Polo hastened back to the Western world with this news—and it was news. For the destiny of a very virile people hung in the balance. Two years later, instead of a hundred, two were sent, and instead of coming to prove that "the way of Christ is best," they brought this: "Become politically and ecclesiastically attached to Rome." Of course, it was turned down—it was too little and too absurd. Then Islam moved into that moral and spiritual vacuum and those Mongols swept across Asia clear to the doors of Europe spreading their conquests and Islam, obliterating many Christian centers, and dooming that part of the world to moral and spiritual sterility. For "Islam always finds a desert or makes one." But, and this is the point, the Christian church had a blurred objective; it presented an offer of being politically and ecclesiastically attached to Rome, neither of which had any real relationship with the request, "to be able to prove that the way of Christ is best."

The request of the Mongols long ago is the central request of today: modern man wants to know "Is the way of Christ the best?" That and that alone is what modern man is wanting the reconstructed church to answer. If it cannot answer that, it has no answer. And the answer must be not just a verbal expression, but also a vital experience. Moreover, it must be both an individual and a corporate experience to be vital.

A verse which is to the point is this one: "Be subject to one another from reverence for Christ" (Eph. 5:21 Moffat). The basis for submitting yourself to one another is what? Because you have to, since you are in a system which demands obedience to higher authority? Or duty demands it? Or "reverence for personality" requires it? All of these fall short. This gives the true motive for submission: "from reverence for Christ." Having submitted to Christ, now you can submit to one another without loss of self-respect. You have made the great submission to Christ; you can now make the lesser submission to each other. For you now submit to each other out of reverence for Christ, for his sake. It is not a mere human submission made because you are compelled to. But it is an expression of your central submission to Christ—you do everything, including this human submission, for his sake. This makes it a noble submission, glorified by the motive of doing it for his sake, instead of an ignoble submission. This leaves you with your head up—it is a privilege. "For his sake" sweetens everything.

Conclusion Number Six: The reconstructed church must go over its emphases and its program and its structure and must eliminate anything comparable to a John Mark issue which is marginal and unimportant and must see that every issue and emphasis in structure and program is central and really Christian—is around Christ himself.

VIII

A FAITH THAT MEN CAN CHANGE AND BECOME REDEMPTIVE

We saw that Barnabas and Paul parted "in irritation" over the question of John Mark and his going with them on a second evangelistic tour. Did this leave permanent sores which refused to heal, or was redemptive grace at work completely healing those sins? Redemptive grace was at work.

The years come and go and Paul, now the aged, is dictating his last letter, Second Timothy. He dictates to his amanuensis this sentence: "Bring John Mark with you for he is profitable to me for the ministry." (2 Tim. 4:11.) I can see the writer lay down his quill, look up at Paul, and smile. Paul, reading its meaning, must have replied: "Yes, I know what you are thinking about—that quarrel that Barnabas and I had over John Mark. Barnabas was a better Christian than I was." (A tear must have trickled down the furrowed cheek of the ancient warrior), "I was hard and unbending and unforgiving. But Barnabas took John Mark, nursed him back to spiritual health, and made a wonderful man out of him. They tell me that John Mark has written a Gospel. God forgive me. Yes, I want him. So write exactly what I say. I really want him and need him." The wound was healed and no scars were left. The mainstream of the Christian movement (Paul) was redemptive again, made so by Paul's saying, "I was wrong—I'm sorry." And by restoring John Mark to his fellowship.

There was a possibility of a permanent rift between Barnabas and Paul solidifying into two denominations: "the Paulites—the Purists" and "the Barnabasites—the Redemptionists." They were two perfectly good ideas, sufficient to make two perfectly good denominations, far better than many modern ideas out of which denominations are formed.

But the denominations were never formed. For Paul and Barnabas both remained Christian. Paul said: "I was wrong—I'm sorry." And Barnabas must have forgiven Paul or else Paul would never have asked for John Mark, not if there had been no reconciliation between the two principals.

The biggest result must have been in Paul and his preaching, for suppose Paul's attitude of not forgiving and not restoring one when he makes a mistake had hardened into a doctrine. The doctrine would have been this: "This is a moral universe. You reap what you sow. You sowed separation from us, now you reap separation from us. The law of karma." Paul would have fallen from grace to karma. So his epistles could never have been written, for they are epistles of grace instead of epistles of karma.

Through Paul the Christian movement remained Christian; through one simple saying: "I was wrong. I'm sorry. Forgive me." Those three sentences of only seven words are the most cleansing compound of words ever put together. It will cleanse any situation, any person, any institution, any nation where it is sincerely uttered. Since we say it to God as a litany, we should practice it as a litany periodically to each other. And it should begin with the pastor and go down through the official boards until saying it become an action, an attitude, and an atmosphere.

The church at Antioch became redemptive because Paul became redemptive. A woman in Korea rapped on the door of a church and asked: "Is this the place where they mend broken hearts?" The answer from within should be: "Yes, we specialize in mending broken hearts, broken homes, broken relationships, broken bodies, and broken hopes. This is our chief business—all else is secondary." The chief business of the church is redemption—the mending of broken everything This refers to the outwardly whole, but inwardly broken, and to the outwardly and inwardly broken. As someone has put it: "It is marvellous what God can do with a broken life if you give him the pieces." The church must specialize in helping people, inside the church and outside the church, to bring the broken pieces and surrender them to God by self-surrender. For self-surrender gathers up the cracked and broken-to-pieces self and surrenders it into the hands of Christ and looks to him to put life together again—on a higher level. And he does just that, to the degree that it is tried.

Take the case of an outwardly whole, but inwardly broken successful pastor and his wife. He had everything—outwardly. He had psychiatric training, an engaging personality, and had had a successful Lutheran ministry in a university setting. What else did he need? An able critic looked at a painting and said: "The conception is excellent, the perspective is correct, the coloring is vivid, everything is fine, except it lacks that!" and he snapped his fingers. This pastor lacked *that*—contagion! He had everything, but he couldn't get it across to others. He came to an Ashram and when he heard of self-surrender, came to see me to clear up certain points about it. After he had cleared these points with me he said, "Thank you, that clears everything," and was about to go when I said: "That clears everything, except one thing. Have you surrendered yourself?" He replied, "Why, no." We got on our knees and he gathered up his inwardly fragmented life and surrendered it to Jesus. A miracle happened. After some months his official board called a meeting to listen to a bill of complaints. They were these: (1) "You have three morning services on Sunday and in none of them can we get our old seats back. Too many students are crowding in. Our regular pattern of placid church life is broken up. It is disturbing." (2) "Is this Lutheran enough?" Before his surrender to God he would have laid them out—they were vulnerable. But now he met criticism with a new spirit that made them wonder and made them want what he had.

Later when I asked him to go to Japan with me for an evangelistic series there, he told his board that he didn't think he could go, too many responsibilities in his church. Their reply: "Whose church is this? It is as much ours as yours. You go, we will pay your salary, and we will pay a pastor to take your place while you are gone. Moreover, the twenty-seven of us here present will pledge ourselves to go out once a week to call on people in visitation evangelism to win them to Christ. You've converted us to what you have found." When he had been made inwardly whole, that wholeness spread to his church and they became a fellowship around surrender to Christ.

But there was one snag—his wife was so inwardly fragmented that she was in the hands of a psychiatrist, suffering with periods of deep depression. She was so negative and fearful of life that she was afraid to lift the telephone receiver to answer a call, afraid she could not handle the demands that would be laid on her. She was saying "No" to everything, including her own life. So one day she went into the cellar to take the pills she had deposited there for just such a crisis. But when she was about to take them, something or Someone wouldn't let her do it.

She, too, came to an Ashram and went through the same surrender to the same victory. When the husband told the psychiatrist what had happened to her, he said he was grateful but added: "But remember her depressions are the recurring kind. They will come back." In the meantime the wife had bounced back from depressions to dancing delight. She was all eagerness to meet life and its demands. She told her husband: "I want to get a college degree." When he asked in surprise, "What course?" she replied, "Russian." This was the toughest subject in the university course. One hundred and eighty-five students entered the course, only five survived, and she was at the top of the five. She was so good she was given a scholarship to go to Russia to speak only Russian for three months. Of the eighteen who were given scholarships from various universities, she was the one to whom everyone came to help solve their problems. She who had been a problem herself now became chief problem-solver.

When her husband called up the psychiatrist and told him that at the end of a year there had been no recurrence of the depressions, he exclaimed: "Well, I'll be d——."

Here was a pastor, his wife, and a congregation—all of them "broken," unfit for the tasks before them. They didn't have what it takes. The pastor was in a rut, the rut of ritual (a rut has been defined as a grave with both ends knocked out). He could perform a ceremony but he couldn't produce a conversion; he could make men a little better but not well.

Another pastor said: "I've been in this church for seven years and I haven't seen God do a thing." He blamed it on God. But it could have been put more accurately: "I have been a pastor of this church for seven years, but I have not seen God do a thing through me." The "through me" was the crux. It was the crux with the pastor we are discussing. He had a good education, a pleasing manner, and no "divine spark." The congregation, complacent and smug, had no expectation and no desire for change, and when a miracle took place in the pastor and hence in those who responded, who pressed in to see this great sight of a Lutheran pastor on fire, the congregation looked on it all as "disturbance." It was a disturbance "upward." The wife was a problem to herself and to everyone else. There was literally no way out of that situation except one—the self-surrender of the pastor. That self-surrender introduced him to the redemptive power of Christ. He walked through that open door. His congregation and his wife followed. The outside student population crowded in to see a pulpit and a church on fire. Psychiatry looked on and saw a place where they were mending broken hearts, broken homes, broken bodies, broken minds, and said: "Well, I'll be d——!"

Here is another case where a husband didn't say anything but silently wept with joy. His wife was empty of everything except fears, negativism, recession, and collapse before life. When she inwardly sagged, her household sagged with her. Her housekeeping went to pieces, her home was a wreck. "Sometimes when my husband came home he would find me crouching behind a chair in the bedroom, afraid of responsibility, afraid of life, just afraid." Then the miracle of change took place. In her own wrecked home she surrendered herself and her problems to Christ. She rose from her knees, looked in the looking glass, and was appalled at what she saw, looked around her room and was further appalled; she went to work, cleaned up her appearance, and cleaned up her home. When her husband came home at the end of the day expecting to have to find his wife crouching behind a chair, he found her at the door when he flung it open and she said with open arms: "Dear, I'm here." Speechless with astonishment at his wife's radiant face, he could only let a silent tear of joy roll down his cheek. He saw a miracle take place before his very eyes—the broken marriage, broken relationship, broken home, broken hope, broken joy, broken everything were suddenly gone and everything suddenly changed. "Is this the place where they mend broken hearts?" Yes, any place is that place when Jesus Christ is there, and he is there when need is there.

But here is the most astonishing miracle in the most astonishing place of all—a drinking party. Mary Fleuty and her husband were confirmed alcoholics at a drinking party of confirmed alcoholics, when she heard a Voice saying to her: "Mary, you will never touch this again." She tremblingly tried to raise the glass in her hand to her lips, but couldn't. Something, or Someone, restrained her. She put her glass down, went over to her husband and said, "Do you know what I heard? A Voice saying, 'You'll never touch this again.' " Her husband replied, "Then if you're not going to touch it again, neither will I." They walked out of that drinking party, and through the woman at the telephone exchange got in touch with a clergyman. But when he heard their story he showed no interest, for they were not of the social class of his congregation, not their kind. The next clergyman they called was interested—they were his kind, they needed redemption. The investment that pastor and his church made in those two seekers after redemption paid off in imponderable dividends. These two made a living by running a mortuary, but more people came to them to find out how to live than how to be buried. Around the clock, alcoholics, drug addicts, people about to be divorced, people just tangled up in general, the unhappy, the despondent came to a mortuary to find out how to live—and found it! One pastor said: "Mary Fleuty leads more people to Christ than the whole United Church of Canada in a given year."

That mortuary is a pattern of what the church is to be: Yes, the church has to bury the dead, but its chief business is to mend broken hearts, broken lives, and broken hopes, and to resurrect the almost-dead and half-alive people.

But the church is to do something else. It is to do what it did to Paul. He went away from Antioch after the quarrel with Barnabas in a legalistic frame of mind: "I was right in not forgiving and in not restoring John Mark to our fellowship." Suppose he had continued that legalistic and moralistic frame of mind and attitude, what would have happened to Paul? Grace would have leaked out of his soul and out of his message and he would have been the legalistic and moralistic Paul, insisting that you must be good if God is to accept you or if I am to accept you. He would have fallen from grace into law. Somewhere along the line Paul pulled his feet out of the flypaper of legalism and put them on the way of grace again.

The redemption from law to grace was seen in a prominent pastor who preached the Gospel of "try harder," of "whip-up-the-will," the Gospel of moralism. Then he saw he was making the wrong emphasis, and inwardly and outwardly he began to emphasize not the whipping-up of the will but the surrender of the will—the acceptance of grace. He was changed and his congregation was changed. The revival was on.

This shift from legalism to redemptive grace is one of the most deeply needed shifts in a reconstructed church. It will be a shift from tense barrenness to effortless fruitfulness, from scraping the bottom of the barrel to relaxed receptivity, and overflowing plenty. It will be a shift from the heavy yoke and burdened duty, to the light yoke and the singing heart, from exhaustion to exhilaration.

Conclusion Number Seven: The reconstructed church is not bogged down in the swamp of legalism, but is on the joyous, contagious way of redemptive love. It believes in people when they cannot believe in themselves and produces the thing it believes in. It takes the rejected and makes them the wanted. It faiths faith out of the faithless, believes belief out of the beliefless and loves love out of the loveless—it is redemptive.

IX

A CHURCH MAKES
ITS LEADERS

When the church at Jerusalem sent Barnabas to Antioch they did more than they knew. Antioch was a lay-founded and a lay-managed church and Jerusalem wisely sent a layman, Barnabas, to direct that church and give what Jerusalem had. But while Barnabas was conscious of what he had to give from Jerusalem, he soon saw that Antioch had some thing to give to Jerusalem. "When he arrived and saw the divine grace at work, he rejoiced." (Acts 11:23 NEB.) He was big enough and great enough to rejoice in the work of another. He didn't pick flaws in what he saw to make a place for himself (the sign of a little man) ; he was big enough to see and to accept and to rejoice in the work of others (the sign of a great-souled man) . So he built on foundations others had laid. But the greatest thing he did was to come to a conclusion and the conclusion was this: "This is the kind of Christian faith I'd like to see Saul exposed to." So he then went off to Tarsus to look for Saul; and when he found him, he brought him to Antioch. (11:25.) Now Saul had gone to Tarsus from Damascus and according to Galatians he had spent fourteen years between Arabia and Tarsus. What doing? Apparently in seclusion. He had heard the call of the Within and had gone into retirement to cultivate that Within. He felt the urge that many in East and West feel, to leave the madding crowd and to meditate and to pray, and to pray and to meditate—to find himself. So Barnabas felt the urge to get Saul back into the stream of Christian life and action. It was the greatest thing he ever did, for Paul left to Tarsus and Arabia would have withered as an ascetic. Barnabas brought him to Antioch and Antioch made Paul. Made him *into* Paul, for it was after his contact with Antioch that Saul became Paul. The word Paul literally means "the little one." He fulfilled the first Beatitude: "How blest are they who know they are poor, the kingdom of heaven belongs to them." He was poor enough to receive, to be receptive, so the Kingdom of Heaven and all its resources belonged to him. "The little one" became the great one, by being poor enough to receive. Antioch taught him receptivity—receptivity to grace. So Antioch made Paul by making him receptive.

As an ascetic he would have earned what he attained by his self-punishment and the rigor of his asceticism. But he learned at Antioch that salvation was not an attainment, but an obtainment through grace—provided you are "little" enough, "poor" enough, to receive. So the church at Antioch produced leaders in its own image—and beyond.

That couldn't have happened at Jerusalem, for the church climate was high and low—leaders and followers, apostles (the sent) and the non-sent. The exception was Stephen, but he was of the lowly too and was given a second-class job—"serving tables," a job beneath the "apostles." He became poor enough to receive, so "the Kingdom of heaven belonged" to him. At Antioch they were all the nobodies who became the somebodies.

The whole church at Antioch fulfilled Jesus' injunction about not using any of these three names. (See Matt. 23:8-13.) First, "Be ye not called rabbi"—those who try to be great by position and learning say: "Listen, wisdom is now speaking." Second, you are not to call anyone 'father' on earth, for one is your heavenly Father—the fathers are those who by age are supposed to be wise. All three of these attitudes are self-assertive, therefore cannot be Christianized. He could trust them with only one name: "Be ye called servants," for the attitude of the servant is self-losing—*diakonos=dia,* "through," plus *konos,* "the dust," the figure of the camel driver who walks through the dust by the camel, while someone else sits on top in the saddle.

The church at Antioch were all deacons—all servers of tables, all who went through the dust. Hence they were the greatest of all. Hence they produced great leaders, among them Paul.

But Paul is not the only one who was in danger of retreating into anonymity. The very setup of the ordinary church tends to produce the anonymous. The congregation is supposed to be silent and receptive and the pastor is supposed to be outgoing and aggressive. That produces by its very makeup the spectator and the participant. By its very makeup it produces the recessive, the ingrown, the noncontributive, and the parasite. Men and women who during the week are molders of opinion, directors of large concerns, directors of destinies are expected to be putty on Sunday, and are supposed to like it. They have little responsibility, hence make little response, except, perhaps, "I enjoyed your sermon." They have little to do, hence they do little.

The church must be re-oriented. The center of gravity in the church must be the laity. If the laity lead they will produce leaders. If the laity only listen they will produce only listeners, but no leaders. If the pastors are the coaches of a team they will produce players. Out of those players they will produce coaches. Out of our present setup is produced increasingly empty pews. If the church is pastor-centered, then the output will be rhetoric; if it is lay-centered, the output will be action. And there will be meaningful discussion around the action. It will be the Word become flesh instead of the Word become word.

If the church drew Paul out of seclusion then Paul drew the

church out of the seclusion of Antioch into universality, into the whole world as its parish.

The biggest redemption before the church today is the rescuing of the laity from church membership as spectatorship to church membership as participationship. Spectatorship is the respectable and the devastating and the getting nowhere except into an eddy in which the bulk of church members have become marooned. They are not bad, they are good, but good-for-nothing. And ushering, taking up collections, greeting people at the door, and sitting on committees do not constitute a job big enough and significant enough to get them out of the eddy, which is going around on itself instead of getting into the mainstream of the Christian movement "where the action is."

A doctor was converted and in his newfound joy went to his pastor and asked for a job through which to express his joy at being a Christian. The pastor replied: "Just what I've been looking for. Could you come on Saturday afternoon and put circulars into envelopes to be mailed?" He responded eagerly, but after several weeks he said to his pastor: "Can't you give me a more significant job than this?" It was a revelation of the church and the demands made on its able membership—doctors putting circulars into envelopes!

Or take this. Here was a businessman, a furniture manufacturer who turned out two thousand tables a day, who, after making enough money, turned to glider flying for avocation and excitement. He trained for five years to get the physical fitness necessary to compete with international glider experts, entered the European competition, and won first prize. The newspapers, commenting on it, said, "The Russians were putty in the hands of Gerald." Later, he heard me in the Sunday Evening Club in Chicago, and his reaction was, "This is reality." He began to read my books, and was converted, really converted. In an Open Heart discussion group he said: "This business of being a Christian is so exciting. There is a surprise around every corner. This is much more exciting than making money, flying gliders, and getting international prizes." When I asked him to take charge of a movement to train laymen in witnessing, in conducting prayer groups, and in teaching spiritual disciplines, he said, "Certainly, it will be exciting." He was out of a backwater eddy into the midstream of vital issues.

Dr. Somerville was an exciting person in his own right—vivacious and vibrant—and he undertook with a group to climb Mount Everest, the highest peak in the world. That was exciting. But not nearly as exciting as to watch him operate, as I have done, on all sorts of pathetic cases in a Mission hospital in South India. In the one case, he was snatching at an invisible laurel—the conquering of Everest—with the eyes of the world on him; in the other, he was stooping over human need and alleviating human pain. This was the more exciting, for as he stooped low he stood higher, higher than Everest, higher than the heavens. In reaching the top of Everest he reached a road with a dead end; in walking into a hospital ward he walked a road with endless vistas of opportunity to help the helpless, to put a song back into songless hearts, and in the process to find his own heart singing. This was where the action was. Climbing Everest was a marooned eddy; climbing a hospital stairs was the mainstream.

The stamp of Paul was upon Antioch, but perhaps more deeply the stamp of Antioch was upon Paul. Here he saw what real Christianity is, and he put what he saw there into many churches he founded. Barnabas made many missionary journeys, but he never made a greater one than when he went from Antioch to look for Paul. And he never did a more effective work of redemption than when he helped redeem Saul, the ascetic marooned at Tarsus, and made him into Paul, the apostle to all the world. That was a seed happening, and what a harvest!

One of the greatest mission fields, if not the greatest, is the church members who are bogged down in their trivialities, producing little or nothing, busy at being busy with little or nothing to show for it. A woman said: "I have lived for seventy years, and I have nothing to show for it." Another: "I have wasted my life in a rat race of social engagements, going everywhere and getting nowhere."

Disraeli, the Jewish Prime Minister of Britain, described himself as "the blank page between the Old and the New Testaments." Whatever Saul (not yet Paul) was doing in the fourteen years spent in Arabia and Tarsus is a blank page between his conversion and his getting into the mainstream of the Christian movement. There is no record that he produced any conversions or any movements, exerted any influence, one way or the other, on human events—he was a blank or at best a blur. After Antioch he left not a blank or a blur, but a mark, the greatest mark on humanity of any human person. And he did it through evangelism.

The great area of redemption for the church is to get possible Pauls—who are caught in the inconsequential, in the second best, in the marginal good and not in the central best—by full surrender to Christ out in the center of the mainstream of a contagious Christianity where things begin to happen, to themselves and to others, and to happen redemptively. This would involve two thirds of the membership of our churches. Two signs could be put up in this "No Man's Land": "Not Really Committed," and "The Greatest Mission Field of the World." Win that group and you win the future.

That group is represented by the Anglican metropolitan of India, Bishop Foss Westcott, who was changed through the Oxford Group Movement. He stood up in one of my meetings in Calcutta and said: "Life began for me at seventy-two." Up to seventy-two, he was an amiable ecclesiast dealing with the secondhand and marginal issues. At age seventy-two, through personal self-surrender he moved from an ineffective eddy in a cove into the mainstream of effective personal and corporate evangelism, and did more in the next ten years than he had done in his whole previous life. For his previous life was prelife. Now his life was linked with Life—he was alive with life. He was living and life-giving.

Conclusion Number Eight: In the church of the future the most important test of its power of survival and of its survival with power will be its capacity to win the two thirds of its membership who are caught in eddies of the inconsequential and the marginal, and are going round and round, getting nowhere and producing little or nothing—except motion. This group is the greatest mission field of the church. It must be changed from a field for evangelism into a force for evangelism.

X

THE CHURCH THAT DOES NOT BEAR OPPOSITION, BUT USES IT

Obviously the church of the future is in for opposition. That opposition will increasingly be a direct and frontal attack on the church, or it will be the type of attack voiced by one of the God-is-dead men when he said: "I don't mention the church for it doesn't matter." In either case the opposition is severe—cold steel, or cold shoulder.

Concerning the latter, the cold-shoulder attitude, it needs little attention. Many who represented the God-is-dead school of thought are now suffering from the cold shoulder themselves. I wrote a chapter in *A Song of Ascents* on the God-is-dead cult. My publishers asked me not to include it, for they said in essence that the God-is-dead cult is itself dead. I asked one of its chief advocates where he got the authority to say that God is dead, did he spin it out of his own imagination? He replied, "Oh, no, I first got it from Nietzsche." I inwardly raised my eyebrows: "A wonderful fountainhead for a religious movement! Nietzsche lived for thirteen years in a madhouse, driven there by his own philosophy of life, and died there." Then I suggested: "Didn't you get it out of your own emptiness of God? Aren't you saying in essence, 'God is dead to me, therefore God is dead?' Now, I agree that God may be dead to you, and if you will say 'God is dead to me,' we will accept it and the whole controversy will be over. But when you say 'God is dead to me, therefore God is dead,' that is bad logic, for you make a single negative into a universal negative. This you have no right to do." Then I asked him if he had helped anyone by advocating this "God is dead" idea? His reply, "I'm not a pastoral counsellor—I'm a theologian," meaning, "No, I haven't helped anyone with my ideas." But a "theologian" of what? A dead God? The God-is-dead theologians are not theologians but morticians, and their "theology" is deomortology. But I'm glad I took out the chapter, for time would have taken it out. Somebody, describing the movement at its source, said: "If a convention of the God-is-dead cult should be held, the adherents could go to it in a Volkswagen and when they returned those who still agreed on what the God-is-dead movement is all about could come back on a motorcycle."

That kind of cold shoulder can be left to time to give what it gives—the cold shoulder. The church is not only cold-shouldered out—the door is shut and sealed. When it gets down to the rising generation it will produce this: A Christian group in a ghetto asked a boy of eight what he wanted for Christmas and the reply came: "I want a charge account and a gun." That is secularism pure and simple. Another: I was looking into a department store window at Christmastime and in the midst of the scenery was a church building. A woman said outloud, "Well, of all things, the church horning in on Christmas."

This is the moral and spiritual atmosphere in which we are to function and operate.

I was dealing with a German doctor who was half fighting what I was presenting and half hungering for it. I gave her a New Testament. She sent it back with a piece of paper wrapped around it with this written on it: "I hate you. Where are you?" That, too, is the mood of the modern man—and woman—half-hating and half-hoping.

The church at Antioch was a church which was so positive that it became persecuted. What did they do when the storm broke upon them? Did they go into hiding underground? No, they went overland, they went everywhere spreading their faith. They didn't bear the persecution—they used it.

Now those who had been scattered by the trouble which arose over Stephen, made their way as far as Phoenicia and Cyprus and Antioch, but they preached the word to none except Jews. Some of them, however, were Cypriotes and Cyrenians, who on reaching Antioch told the Greeks also the gospel of the Lord Jesus; the strong hand of the Lord was with them, and a large number believed and turned to the Lord. (Acts 11:19-21 Moffatt.)

So the Antiochian group were in an ambivalent situation—some fighting back in persecution and some fighting to get what these persecuted people possessed. Without the persecution they might have settled down to half allegiance and to a noncontagious type of Christian faith. The winds of persecution filled the sails of their souls, and they took the rudder and made those winds drive them to islands and lands of need. The persecution persecuted them into productivity. It cost them something to be Christian and it meant something.

We are entering, or have entered, a similar situation in the world. We are not being hunted and driven from place to place by outer persecution, but we are being hunted and driven from position to position by the theological and philosophical and the moral and immoral storms that beat upon the Christian position from every direction—North, East, South, West—and from below. Only heaven is left open to us. Can we get enough inspiration and power from that open direction augmented by the winds that blow from the four corners of the earth which, while they seemingly oppose us, are really crying out for the very things we stand for in the Christian faith? In other words, are not many of these winds saying: "I hate you. Where are you?" And are not many winds saying in essence: "If you can't convert me, I'll sue you for breach of promise? Why don't you do what you are called to do, convert us?" In other words, can we not merely bear this hour, but *use* it as our hour of greatest opportunity?

The church must not merely get through this hour and the future hours somehow, but triumphantly. It must fulfill the last of Toynbee's attitudes which nations and movements can take when they face a crisis that demands decision: First, the church can retreat into the past, and glory in what the nation or the movement has been. Toynbee calls that archaism. Second, the church may leap over into the future and build castles in the air, dream of what it will do. He calls that futurism. Third, the church may retreat within and give itself to mystical experiences. He calls that the retreat within. All these are in lieu of decisions in the crisis. Fourth, the church may take hold of the crisis, transform it into a higher type with a fresh beginning. He calls that transformation. Only the last, transformation, survives. The rest perish.[1] The Chinese have a word for crisis, made up of two characters—"danger and opportunity." In every crisis there are these two possibilities—danger that things may go down into a crash and opportunity that things may be transformed into a higher level.

Those two possibilities are before the church today—danger that we may retreat into yesterday and be of yesterday, looking back. Or we may try to leap into the future and daydream without decisive decision. We may retreat within into mystic experiences without any facing of the crisis demanding decision. Only as the church lays hold of resources from above to fend off the attacks made upon us, and to win those who while attacking us are really crying out for what we have, can we survive and survive with power—transforming power in the individual and in society.

To ask the church not to bear this crisis but to use it is to call the church to a manifestation of its central genius. For the

[1] Arnold Toynbee, *An Historian's Approach to Religion* (New York: Oxford University Press, 1956), pp. 81-82.

Christian faith doesn't promise to exempt its followers from sorrow and unmerited pain, nor does it explain them. It does something much more radical—it teaches us to take hold of the worst and turn it into the best, to take hold of a Calvary and turn it into an Easter morning. Jesus didn't bear the cross, he used it. The cross was sin and he turned it into the healing of sin; the cross was hate and he turned it into redemptive love; the cross was man at his worst and Jesus, through it, showed God at his redemptive best. He turned the worst into the best. The church today is in essentially the same position as the early church—it is persecuted. Not with spearpoints, but with more deadly jibes: "outmoded," "a relic," "unrelated," "unneeded," "irrelevant." These hurt more than bayonets and daggers. What do they do to us? Sting us into retreat, or sting us into action? If we are true to our faith they will sting us into action. For none of those names fit the Christian movement when the Christian movement is Christian. So this opposition should drive us back to Christ and his Kingdom though we have wandered far from them. It is not enough to go back to Christ, for Christ without his Kingdom is a sovereign without a state, a ruler without a realm—in this case a universal ruler without a universal realm.

When I had my first contact with our archenemy Marxian communism in 1934, I was stunned by the impact. The three answers God gave me have remained with me as the valid and vital answers after thirty-six testing years. The three things I needed were: an unshakable kingdom, an unchanging person, and both as realism. And what I needed the church needs today, and the reconstructed Church must have if it is to survive. To be specific:

1. I rediscovered the Kingdom of God. When I saw the Communists building up a new order without God and doing it enthusiastically, with young people carrying earth out of a subway and chanting, "We are making a new world, we are making a new world"—I was stunned. I needed reassurance. I went to

my New Testament one morning in Moscow and got it. This verse arose out of my morning devotions: "Let us be grateful for receiving a kingdom that cannot be shaken." (Heb. 12:28 RSV). It not only reassured me, it possessed me. I saw that there was one unshakable kingdom and that was the Kingdom of God. The kingdom of communism is shakable. They have to hold it together by force. Relax the force, and it disintegrates. The kingdom of capitalism is shakable. Eisenhower, while president, had a heart attack and the stock market dived four billion dollars. The kingdom of health is shakable. The doctor shakes his head at the end of an examination and says: "You've got a cancer," and your kingdom of health collapses. Everything earthly is shakable. But there is one Kingdom—and only one—that not only will not be shaken, but cannot be shaken. For it is ultimate reality—a "kingdom built from the foundation of the world"—a kingdom built *into* the foundations of the world. If you live according to that kingdom the sum total of reality is behind you. You have cosmic backing. Step out of that kingdom and you have nothing behind you—nothing but you. You are shakable—very shakable, so shakable that you will probably have to live on barbiturates. As one doctor put it: "You ministers must raise the level of faith, so we doctors can lower the level of barbiturates." Or as one nurse put it: "We are being transformed into a nation of imbeciles through tranquilizers." We are increasingly nervous because nothing is behind us—nothing but our own shaky selves.

Man needs nothing, absolutely nothing, so much as he needs to feel that he belongs to an unshakable kingdom—the Kingdom of God.

2. I rediscovered the unchanging person. The morning after I was shocked into the unshakable Kingdom I went back to my New Testament eager for more. I found it. This verse arose and spoke to my condition: "Jesus Christ is the same yesterday, today, and for ever." (Heb. 13:8 RSV.) In a changing, uncertain world do we have an unchanging person—and is that person

Jesus Christ? The answer is certain: Yes, Jesus Christ is the only unchanging Person, "the same, yesterday, today, and for ever." A Hindu historian put it this way: "My study of history has shown me that there is a moral pivot in the world and the best life of East and West is revolving more and more around that moral pivot. That moral pivot is the person of Jesus Christ. There is nobody else bidding for the heart of the world. There is no one else on the field." There is literally "no one else on the field"—the rest are pitifully outclassed.

So I came out of Russia with two things in my mind and heart—an unshakable kingdom and an unchanging person, the absolute order and the absolute person. The two have now become one. The absolute order, the Kingdom of God, and the absolute person, the Son of God, have coalesced. Jesus used interchangeably "for the Kingdom's sake" and "for my sake." He was the Kingdom embodied. To have a relationship with him is to have relations with the Kingdom embodied in him. That made relations with him both individual and social, not now individual and now social, but by their very nature both at once and at the same time. This Kingdom-person lays his hands on the individual will and says: "Repent, submit, and be converted—obey"; and lays his hands upon the collective will and says the same: "Repent, submit, and be converted and obey."

Humanity needs and, down deep, wants, if it only knew it, just exactly what the Christian faith offers, namely, a personalized absolute order, which when obeyed totally brings total freedom and total fulfillment. If humanity needs anything more or anything other than this, I haven't heard of it, nor can I imagine it. I say this after scanning the horizons of the world in East and West for over half a century.

But a doubt lingers: This may be true ideally but what about really? Is this unrelated idealism, or is it solid realism? This leads me to the third thing Russia bumped me into discovering; that is, the discovery of Christianity as realism instead of idealism. I was on a train in Russia when a Russian actress said to me: "I suppose you are a religious man?" When I said that I was, she replied: "You are religious because you are weak. You want God to comfort you, to hold your hand." My reply: "My friend, you are mistaken. I don't want God to hold my hand, I want him to strengthen my arm that I might reach out a helping hand to others. I don't want religion as comfort. I want it as adequacy for whatever happens." Seeing she was on the wrong track, she said: "Well, I suppose you are an idealist?" More hesitatingly, I replied: "Yes, I suppose I am." "Goodbye, *au revoir*, I'm a realist," she waved me away with a flick of the hand. Communism was realism, Christianity was idealism! It set me to thinking. I went to the New Testament to see whether I was an idealist or a realist. I spent two years there and emerged a confirmed realist. I saw that Jesus was a realist—he was the Word become flesh. Everything he taught was realized in him.

A pastor writes today: "I was reading one of your books *Is the Kingdom of God Realism?* when I sat in a lunch counter in Chicago on my way to work. When I read in your book that the Christian life is the normal, natural way to live and the only happy and healthy way to exist, all of a sudden something seemed to 'click' in my life. For some reasons, I had always held the idea that as a Christian I was more or less out of step. Now the whole universe seemed to come into its proper place. I left the restaurant walking on air. I felt I belonged to God's world—that the world belonged to me. I shall never forget that holy moment, one of the greatest of my life."

Suppose that "holy moment" of realization should become widespread, should possess the church—the holy moment when it would realize that all outside the Kingdom are out of step, are living against the grain of the universe, and that only those who are within the Kingdom are unshakable and all outside the Kingdom are shakable and are on the road to futility and decay; that "every plant which my Father hath not planted shall be rooted up." Then and then only would we face the world with a sense of conviction, a sense that no matter what the position is now we are on the winning side and everything will come out at his feet. Then instead of shaking we would shake the world.

A very intelligent Roman Catholic woman in charge of an important program on television said to me before we went on the air: "I am a new Catholic. I am at war with my Pope over birth control. At first I felt a sense of freedom. I had formerly said to my church, 'You are infallible, I put myself into your hands. You tell me what to do.' Now I was standing on my own feet—free. But soon came a sense of insecurity. My infallibility was gone and with it my security. I am shaken and insecure." When we went on the air, she asked me what was my main emphasis in speaking to America. I told her and the TV audience: "It is a double emphasis, but one: the unshakable Kingdom—'Let us be grateful for receiving a kingdom that cannot be shaken'; and the unchanging person—'Jesus Christ, the same yesterday, today and forever'—the absolute order and the absolute person!" She saw the significance of that at once and said: "Then you have an infallibility." "Yes," I replied, "and it is not built up, it is built in—built into reality, is reality, is therefore unshakable." "Then, tell me about it." She was all eagerness, and followed me to the door. She represents the shaken modern person, seeking security in the midst of a shaken modern world, seeking infallibility in a world of relative values. I was glad I could present an infallibility which was not Protestant or Catholic, but Christian, and that she could have it as a Catholic if she would take it. It belonged to us both—for the taking!

I love the certainty of a sticker on a car in which a young couple were driving: "If your God is dead, try mine. My God is alive."

A college professor said to his students: "Young men, play the game of life." "But," put in a student, "what if there is nothing to shoot at—there are no goalposts?" Our reply to the confused and doubting student is simple: "We have goalposts—they are these: the unshakable Kingdom and the unchanging person. If you shoot between those two you will always be on target."

In this period when everything that *can* be shaken *is* being shaken, the church has its greatest opportunity. Here we can stand with an unshakable kingdom and an unchanging person over against the weak relativisms of the day, and can confront them with no hesitations. In other words, we should not bear the oppositions of this hour but use them.

Conclusion Number Nine: The Christian faith is founded on the cross. The cross is defeat and you cannot defeat defeat; you cannot break brokenness. It turns the defeat of calvary into the Victory of Easter morning. Jesus didn't bear the cross, he used it. So opposition becomes opportunity. This opposition can help us cleanse our wrongs, realign our scattered energies—realign them to vital issues; squeeze out the irrelevant in our lives and programs and leave only the relevant.

XI

THE CHURCH
THAT LISTENS TO GOD

The center of the life of the church of today, both liberal and conservative, is the Sunday morning service. Around that Sunday morning service the life of the church revolves. Take that out and there isn't much left. The biggest crowd assembles for it, the greatest preparation goes into it, the greatest expectancy centers there. If anything happens, it happens there. For this is the one and only contact the church has with a majority of its members, and it is the one and only contact that the majority of members have with the church. It is the nerve center of the church. If any message or life impulses go out into the body of the church, it goes out from there.

Now some of the advocates of the secularization of the church are saying that the center of the life of the church should not be in the Sunday worship. It should be shifted from there to the uplift of the ghetto—to the abolition of poverty and to the raising of the life of the ghetto in general, largely economic. In other words, the center of life in the church should not be in God, but in man. To serve man is to worship God. Or in many minds you may now leave out the worship of God and serve man only. So the reply of Jesus to the last temptation of the devil: "Thou shalt worship the Lord thy God and him only shalt thou serve" is changed into "Thou shalt give up the worship of the Lord thy God and man only shalt thou serve." In other words, a humanism results.

But does a humanism result? If you lose God do you find man? I believe if God fades out, man will fade out too. You cannot believe long in man unless you believe in something more than man that gives worth, values, meaning to man, in spite of his sin and capacity to blunder. Someone has defined democracy as "that madness which believes that which isn't true, namely, that man can govern himself. And yet without that belief man will never become what we believe him to be." But it has been proven that democracy cannot exist without a basis of character which Christianity produces. A chief minister of an Indian state, a Hindu, in introducing me, said: "Our problem is now different. Once it was to gain our freedom, now it is to retain our freedom. For the retaining of our freedom we need character. There is no doubt that the impact of Jesus Christ on the framework of human life produces miracles of changed character and as such we welcome that impact." Mr. S. Kurusu, the special envoy to America sent to try to head off the war between Japan and America, said: "Japan will never become a democracy until Japan becomes Christian."

The impact of Jesus upon the framework of human nature has produced more humanism than all the humanists of the centuries put together. It was no mere chance that he was called the Son of man, for wherever he goes the sons of men lift up their heads and their hopes. A leper said to me: "Everybody said to me 'Go,' but only Jesus said to me 'Come.' " One Bible version said Jesus was a "light to lighten the Gentiles," but another says he was "a light to unveil the Gentiles"—to unveil the possibilities of the Gentiles. And what possibilities he has unveiled!

And nothing "unveils" human possibilities so much as worshiping the Lord, especially if that worship is characterized by listening rather than speaking. For when we listen, the Lord speaks. So the account says, "As they were worshipping the Lord and fasting, the Holy Spirit said, 'Come! set me apart Barnabas and Saul for the work to which I have called them' " (Acts 13:2 Moffatt). Here worship was listening as well as praising. It is comparatively easy and cheap to praise God, for in doing so we offer to him our words, but in listening we offer to him ourselves—we offer our obedient selves to do what he says. So praising God is cheap and verbal—listening to God is expensive—and vital. So without listening, worship becomes verbal and formal and we become "drunk with the wine of our own wordiness." But in listening we hear a call to act, to undertake, to adventure, to go forward. This church at Antioch did its greatest work in listening while worshiping. For the Holy Spirit said: "Come! Set me apart Barnabas and Saul for the work to which I have called them." Into that moment the destiny of continents was packed. For Barnabas and Saul started the greatest movement that ever touched our planet. They introduced into Asia and Europe directly, and into the rest of the world indirectly, the greatest redemptive movement that has ever come to humanity. Nothing else can be compared to it. It is in a class by itself, incomparable. "The men who have turned the world upside down have come hither," said the discerning when Paul and Barnabas came to their city. They did turn that world upside down, and for the better. For the movement they introduced was the most purifying, the most regenerative, the most life- and society-changing which has ever been introduced into the human race. And it still is.

The Christian faith has many critics but no rivals in the work of human redemption. There isn't a spot on earth where they have allowed us to go where we haven't brought schools, hospitals, leper and blind asylums, churches—everything to lift the soul, the mind, the body of the race. No other movement has done anything like it. So with all its faults the church is the greatest serving institution on earth. And all of this came out of listening to God.

The church at Antioch listened to God and the world listened to them. If the church doesn't listen to God and get its guidance through him then the world, including its own members, will turn to the stars for guidance—to astrology. As if lumps of matter floating in space could give guidance to rational human beings! That is materialism, pure and simple. The Greek mind was creative until the dead hand of astrology took it over and ruined it. The Hindu mind is a very acute mind and deeply philosophical, but its feet are not on earth, for it is gazing at the stars for guidance. And now it has invaded the Western world. Five million people in America get guidance for their lives from horoscopes printed in the daily newspapers. Of all the silly and life-destroying things newspapers publish, this horoscope business is the silliest and most life corroding. It is a sign of decay. For if one has lost his nerve to make moral judgments and decisions, he turns to the stars and lets them decide for him. In India a Hindu told me he was about to travel, looked up his horoscope and found it was not an auspicious time to travel; he waited an hour till the time was auspicious and rushed to the train, "but alas, the train pulled out without me." Auspicious time, but he missed his train. If an individual or nation waits for auspicious or inauspicious times, the train of progress will pull out without them!

The head of education in an Indian state, a Hindu, would not move out of or come into his house unless a kite (a hawk common in Indian cities) were flying in an auspicious direction. Head of education and tied up with that! But it is no worse than America tied up with astrology.

Then if people do not get guidance from God they will turn to the dead for guidance—turn to spiritualism. I cannot remember hearing or reading of a single out-of-the-ordinary or particularly wise statement ever being credited by the spiritualists as coming from the dead. One woman quoted to me a statement she heard Jesus uttering when he introduced Rufus Moseley to her: "I am introducing to you the Right Reverend Rufus Moseley." This from behind a curtain. Knowing Rufus Moseley as I do, I cannot imagine this apostle of simplicity and reality being introduced as "Right Reverend." Brother Rufus would burst out laughing at the absurdity. And knowing Jesus as I do, I question whether there will be any "Right Reverends" in heaven. There will be just redeemed people.

But people want guidance. I believe God guides individuals and groups in five ways. First, the life and teaching and character of Jesus are our general guidance. For he is the revelation of what God is like and what man can be like. In his own person he is the revelation of God and man. He is therefore our general guidance. God could not guide you to do anything that is un-Christlike. He would violate his own nature and character. So suspect any guidance that doesn't fit in with the character and life and teaching of Jesus. When in doubt, do the most Christlike thing and you won't go wrong.

Second, he guides through the counsel of good people—by a luminous word, a helpful suggestion, detached advice, and the way is clearer. Not clear, for the choice is always ours. We may listen to people but the final decision is always ours before God.

Third, he guides through opening providences, some need which we can fill, and that need may be a call.

Fourth, through our own heightened moral intelligence: "Can you not of yourselves judge that which is right?" said Jesus. He expected his disciples to be mature enough to come to mature and right moral judgments.

Fifth, he guides through the inner voice. When these other four ways are not available or are not clear enough he speaks directly to us. Through an outer audible voice? No, through the framing of the words within the mind, just as when we talk with ourselves the words frame themselves within the mind without being audible. How can we distinguish between the voice of the subconscious and the voice of God? The voice of the subconscious argues with you to try to convince you. The voice of God doesn't argue; it speaks, and the words are self-verifying. You feel it is real and it is.

The psalmist writes: "He that made the eye shall he not see? He that made the ear shall he not hear?" And we may add: He that gave us power to communicate with each other shall he not communicate with us? And he does—individually and collectively. The greatest decisions of my life have been made through the inner voice. And that inner voice has always been right, except on two occasions when I mistook the voice of the subconscious as the voice of God. They turned out wrong, for I was emotionally involved. I wanted it to happen. But two mistakes in fifty years of the voice being always right can be absorbed. The outcomes have proved it.

This church at Antioch heard collectively the voice of the Holy Spirit at the time of prayer and worship: "Separate me Barnabas and Saul for the work to which I have called them." They were so attuned to each other and to God that they could hear the voice of God collectively. That this voice and this listening were authentic was authenticated by the outcome. As I write this near Cape Kennedy, Florida, with the country in expectancy over three men attempting tomorrow to go to the moon and back, I contrast in my thinking the two journeys. One costing billions of dollars and watched by many millions of men to get three men to circumvent an uninhabited dead body—the moon, and get back again; and the other, the setting out of two men on foot, with a handful to see them off, but with a strange burning in their hearts, to share with Asia and Europe and eventually the world the miraculous Good News of Jesus Christ. I contrast these two setting outs and their ultimate outcomes. The ultimate outcome when the three men got back safely was that they had seen at firsthand the craters and potholes in the dead body. The result was a landing on a dead body—but landing there first! Ahead of Russia. A cosmic child's game—"I got there first!" A dead end!

But these two men with only two walking sticks as outer support had a strange fire burning within them and started the greatest movement in human history. For they did not gaze at craters in a dead moon, they looked into the eyes of living men who thirsted for truth and for redemption from what they were. They invested their lives in living people, not in dead craters and tinselled glory, and the people by the millions responded and a new era began—an era of hope and change and redemption. They introduced into society a divine leaven which is leavening the whole world, and ultimately the whole lump of humanity will be leavened—or perish! For it is proving the one hope of humanity—it is that or futility and decay.

Will the regenerated church learn this lesson? Will it learn to listen to God corporately, get his guidance, and rise up with a sense of mission and direction, saying, "God wills it"? Then we will discern between the trivial and the tremendous, the marginal and the central, the irrelevant and the relevant, the commonplace and the consequential.

I pressed a button in Santiago, Chile, the southernmost U.S. tracking station for satellites, and a message went to Tyros VI, a weather satellite in the South Pacific, fifteen hundred miles away and going at the rate of eighteen thousand miles an hour. I told it to take pictures in thirty-two minutes of the weather conditions over Australia and send them to Washington where they would be teletyped to Santiago. In two minutes word came back by the wiggling of the indicator that my message had been received and my orders would be carried out. I did not even wait for the reply, for I knew it would say "Cloudy" or "Clear." All that for that!

I pressed a "button" in a man's heart as he sat in an auditorium in St. Louis. He had spent $65,000 on pagan psychiatrists in trying to straighten himself out. They interpreted twelve hundred dreams to untangle his subconscious, but he rather grew worse. He was spiritually and physically down and out. But as I pressed that button the message he got was this: "Let us be thankful that we receive a kingdom which cannot be shaken." I pressed the right button. He listened, opened his heart, said to himself, "This is it, my quest is over."

He walked out of all his problems, became one of the most integrated and dedicated persons I ever knew. He left his millions for pressing the button of the unshakable Kingdom in hearts everywhere, through a "Laymen's Trust for Evangelism." Pressing that button in a shattered businessman's heart was big business. When I pressed that button in Santiago, I got back the answer "Clear" or "Cloudy." When I pressed that button in St. Louis, I got back the reply: "Redeemed and redeeming—forever." Listening to God is big business—the biggest business on this planet. Beside it the highest achievement is comparatively trivial.

But suppose a whole church would listen to God? What for? Words of comfort and communion? No, words that were marching orders: "Separate me Barnabas and Saul for the work for which I have called them." "For the work." The comfort and the communion would be a by-product of carrying out that "work." God is creating billions of tons of new matter every day, so they tell us. That is comparatively easy for God. But he has the more complicated and difficult job of re-creating billions of free-willed beings who have gone astray. He cannot coerce them, for coerced goodness is not goodness. They must consent. And he asks our help in this "work"—the "work" of pressing buttons inside wistful and waiting and rebellious hearts—buttons which bring the Good News: Not "earn a kingdom," or "be good enough for a kingdom," but "receive"—receive it as a gift. But a "gift" which, if you receive it, makes you belong to the giver forever. Who wouldn't belong to such an unshakable kingdom, an unshakable kingdom which gives you perfect freedom, freedom to live, to create, and to develop forever. Everybody wants that, if they only knew it! We are to press buttons that tell people that this is what they want!

I mentioned an intelligent, honest-minded, confused, and empty young woman standing at the door of the most modern of institutions—the TV studio—and wistfully saying, "Do come again and tell about your built-in infallibility." This is a picture of this modern age, its freedom turned to uncertainty and confusion. They cannot stand this emptiness. They stand between two worlds—one dead and the other not yet born.

But that world of uncertainty and confusion will not listen to us as Christians unless we listen to God. A caretaker, when asked by the pastor why he didn't attend church service, replied: "Have you had any fresh news from God?" The listening church will have fresh news from God.

Suppose on Sunday morning ten minutes were set aside for the audience to listen to God, listen to what God would say in answer to the question: "What would you have us as individuals and as a collective body to do?" Then have a church meeting to prayerfully listen to the suggestions that emerge. It would bring a sense of expectancy into the Sunday morning service. Now we listen to a sermon from man and leave it at that. And that is the result—it is left at that, nothing happens.

In order to produce a listening congregation, small groups for prayer and fellowship and listening to God may be the training ground for corporate listening in a church. I know of a church where there are seventeen of these prayer and listening groups. They are the training ground for collective praying and listening. The total impact is tremendous.

As I mentioned in *A Song of Ascents* I have a personal listening post. As one gets older he usually awakens earlier. I decided to put a listening post in that blank early morning space. Instead of tossing restlessly, trying to get back to sleep, I fill it with a quiet listening: "Have you anything to say to me—I'm listening." Often he lays it on the line: "You had better change this and this." And my reply: "Wait till morning and I'll do it." But once when I asked if he had anything to say, he replied: "No, I love you, go to sleep." But as I look back I find that the greatest decisions of my life and the most productive have come out of the listening post. For instance, this assurance came out of the listening post: "You are mine, life is yours." Again at seventy: "I am giving you the best years of your life so far—the next ten

years." They have been undoubtedly so. When I neared eighty
I proposed asking the Father for an extension of another ten
years. But he beat me to it in these words at the listening post:
"And now begins the era of the greatest contribution you have
known." Six of those years have come and gone and they have
been the most contributive six years of my life—more fruitful,
more constructive, and more contributive in general—so far!

Does this guidance include the social: I had just finished the
National Christian Mission, which was intensely personal in its
demand for conversion. I was awakened about four o'clock in a
hotel in Los Angeles with this voice: "I want you here. I want
you here." I pleaded that my work was done here in America, I
must go back to India for the present. But the voice was insistent, so I cancelled my flights. It was the call to try to head off
the Japanese-American War. It was one of the most fruitful
periods of my life. It resulted in failure, but it was a call of
God—very social.

I have just returned from a cataract operation in the hospital
here in Boston. As I neared the operation my inner voice repeated this: "The best, the best, the best ahead, including your
eyesight." If I belong to Christ, life belongs to me. I can rescue
something good out of everything that happens—life belongs to
me.

To the degree the church listens to God and obeys, the people will listen to the church and will obey its Lord.

We must go back to the Bible, but we must go forward in
listening and obeying "what the Spirit says to the churches" and
to your church in particular for today in today's environment.
Then we will answer the question of the caretaker: "Have you
any fresh news from God?" We *will* have fresh news from God
and it will be *the Good News*—up-to-date for today, and relevant.

Conclusion Number Ten: Jesus said: "I have still much to
tell you but you cannot bear it at present. However when the
Spirit of truth comes he will lead you into all the truth. . . .

He will draw upon what is mine and disclose it to you" (John 16:12-14 Moffatt). *Here he provided for a continuing revelation based upon the revelation revealed in himself but further applied. The church must listen for that continuing revelation which the Spirit of truth brings and apply it to present problems and situations. It must be a listening church and an obeying church.*

XII

WHAT DID GOD SAY THEN AND WHAT DOES HE SAY NOW?

We come now to a crucial element in the life of the reconstructed church. We have seen that the church in Antioch had
embodied universalities.

Now a church which had such vital things in it would seem,
in our eyes, a very Christian and a very dynamic church. Fulfilling those vital things it would seem to be a Christian church.
But it was not, not until it heard and heeded its crowning
function—evangelism. When God spoke to that church as they
listened together, what word did he speak? Evangelism! "Separate me Paul and Barnabas for the work to which I have called
them." These two men represented the outward thrust, the
thrust of evangelism into that ancient pagan world. That was
God's highest and most climactic word: Evangelism! When
they listened to and obeyed that word that church fulfilled its
highest and most vital function. Without that fulfillment the
church itself would have been unfulfilled. If it had fulfilled all
the other things and had left out evangelism, its heart would
have ceased to beat; it would have been a body without a
heartbeat—a corpse. Paul and Barnabas became the church at
Antioch taking sandals and walking into that confused and
decaying ancient world—a world that was needing exactly what
Paul and Barnabas brought, the Good News of Jesus Christ.

Will God's voice to the church today be different than it was when he spoke to the church at Antioch? Has the world so changed and the age become so different that we need some other word? Or is human nature fundamentally the same and the need of that human nature fundamentally the same? That ancient world had lost its nerve, was decaying, the old sanctions were losing their grip, men were groping, and were inwardly empty. The same can be said of today. Men are groping and empty. The modern man stands between two worlds—one dead and the other not born. And he cannot stand this emptiness. That emptiness, according to Jung, is "the central neurosis of our time." Man needs conversion—man as man needs conversion.

Not proselytism. Jesus was opposed to proselytism. "You compass land and sea to gain a proselyte and when you gain him you make him twofold more a child of hell than yourselves," said Jesus to the Jewish leaders of that day. For proselytism is the coming over from one group to another group without any necessary change in character or life. It is a change of label and not of life. He saw it was a corporate egoism which wanted to add to collective power and prestige by numbers. It was essentially an irreligious process. But Jesus insisted on conversion: "Except ye be converted and become as little children you cannot enter the Kingdom of God." "Except a man be born again he cannot see the Kingdom of God." Conversion is a profound change in character and life, followed by an outer change which corresponds to that inner change. It is the business of religion, the chief business, to produce conversion. And when it can no longer do so it has lost its right to be called Christian. Its sanctions may be ancient, its liturgy ornate, its preaching eloquent, and the setting worshipful, but if it has no power to convert weak men into strong men, impure men into pure men, self-centered men into Christ-centered men— no power to convert, it is all this side of the Christian faith.

It is sub-Christian, no matter how often it names the name of Christ.

Dr. Radhakrishnan, a Hindu philosopher and ex-president of India, said to me: "John the Baptist tried to make men better. Jesus made men different—one was reformation, the other regeneration." A British psychiatrist said: "Man is made for conversion." And until he is converted he is not a normal man—he is subhuman.

Three quarters of the opposition to the church comes from disappointment with the church—disappointment that the church hasn't power to convert men to make them different, not merely better but different. People flock to the churches which can and do convert them and desert the churches which cannot.

When the Constitution of India was being debated, the question of "the right to profess, practice and propagate one's faith is guaranteed" was up. Many Hindus gagged over "propagate." But a Hindu arose and said, "To propagate one's faith is an integral part of the Christian's faith, so if you do not give the Christians the right to propagate you do not give them the right to profess and practise, for they cannot profess and practise if they do not propagate." That observation carried the day. If those three things were as deeply rooted in the Christian mind as they were in the Hindu's mind, it would produce a more virile type of Christianity. For if there is no propagating, there is no professing or practicing. Nothing is ours until we share it. It is a law of the mind that that which is not expressed dies. All expression deepens impression. Impression minus expression equals depression.

Here at the place of conversion we can unite. I said to the Archbishop of Peru: "How would it do to have the Catholics and the Evangelicals of Peru to renounce proselytism and join together on conversion—there is nothing that Peru needs more than conversion. Unite to produce conversion, leaving it open for the converted to join any church he may choose." He said, "I would welcome that cooperation."

The President of India, Mr. Giri, a very noble person, said to me: "During the last seventeen years there have been two casualties—character and integrity. We are headed for disaster unless we can get them back." This is the need of East and West—every man's need.

Harnack, the church historian, says: "All the early conquests of Christianity were carried on by informal missionaries." Everybody who received the Gospel gave the Gospel. If one receives the Gospel and doesn't give the Gospel what one has turns out to be less than the Gospel and other than the Gospel. For the very nature of that Gospel is "Freely ye have received, so freely give." So if you do not give you haven't got.

Jesus said a profound thing when he said this: "There is nothing covered that shall not be revealed, hidden that shall not be made known." He was saying that it is the nature of life to reveal itself—the within becomes the without. So if there is no without there will soon be no within. If the reply is made that the Christian within can reveal itself in deeds instead of words, the answer is that this is a half-truth. Suppose Jesus, who is the Word become flesh, had said to himself: "I'll be the Word become flesh only—I'll let them see what I am by what I do alone, not at all by what I say." That would have been a half-revelation. For if the outer without the inner is hypocrisy, so the inner without the outer is also hypocrisy. The total person should express the total life and life is made up of words as well as deeds. The words and the deeds both reveal. Suppose he had only revealed himself through deeds without the revelation through his words; the revelation would have been like a bird trying to fly with one wing. Words and deeds are the two wings of the Christian as he soars and sings.

So when people tell me they belong to "the right wing" or to "the left wing," it leaves me cold. I want to belong to both wings in equal balance. So those who call for deeds only and those who call for words only are both wrong. I want to belong to him whose words were deeds and whose deeds were words—both in a living blend. "Never man spoke like this Man," for never man lived like this man. You can't tell where his words end and his deeds begin, or his deeds end and his words begin, for his words were deeds and his deeds were words —they were one.

Now do not misunderstand me—I believe in the abolition of the ghetto and the abolition of poverty. The first two items of the Kingdom manifesto of Jesus were: "Good news to the poor" and "release to the captives." We usually make this the spiritually poor—but it doesn't say so, it says "the poor." Good news to the poor would be that there should be no poor. And release to the captives is usually taken to mean politically captive, but a more widespread captivity is to be found in the socially, racially, and economically captive in the slums and ghettoes of the world. They are a standing disgrace to the civilizations of the world—a ramshackle monument to our selfishness. So it is an integral part of the Christian program to get rid of both.

Suppose the church at Antioch had fastened on food relief, when they sent the first relief expedition to Jerusalem, and had said: "Poverty is the main evil, we will center on that. Evangelism is verbal, this is vital. This shall be our main emphasis." Suppose the church had made food relief and the abolition of poverty the center of its message and suppose they had succeeded in abolishing hunger and poverty, would men have still needed conversion? The answer is our present age: We have succeeded in abolishing poverty among 90 percent of the people of America in this affluent age. Do those 90 percent need conversion? The doctors' offices, the psychiatrists' couches, the breakdown in morals, not merely in the slums, but in the houses of the well-to-do, in the all-pervasive emptiness and confusion of modern affluent man—all these facts point to the necessity of conversion in the high and low and middle brackets—man as man needs conversion. And this is in East and West.

When Jesus said "Ye must be born again. . . . except a man be born again he cannot see the kingdom of God," he was talking to a ruler of the Jews. Not to "the down-and-outs" but to "the up-and-on-tops." And when he said: "Except ye be converted and become as little children you cannot enter the kingdom of heaven," to whom was he speaking? To his own disciples, who were disputing over who was greatest in the kingdom of God. Disciples needed conversion when their egos began to assert themselves.

At the close of a luncheon engagement for the bankers of Wall Street, one of these big businessmen asked me where I was to go next, and when I told him, he said: "I'd like to take you in my car." We hadn't gone half a block when he asked: "How do you get what you are talking about?" When I replied: "Can I tell you going through the roaring traffic of this city?" He replied: "There is no other place—we will have to." I replied: "You watch the traffic and I'll talk." I talked to him about self-surrender and felt he was responding. So I asked whether we could pray going through that traffic. He replied: "I'd like you to pray, but I'll have to watch the traffic." "You watch and I'll pray." I'm not sure but what I kept my own eyes open! But we met Christ—this living Christ, right in the midst of that roaring traffic. When I got out at the place where I was to speak, he grabbed my hand in both of his and said with deep emotion: "Thank you, I'm in." "In" the unshakable kingdom—by conversion!

If laymen need conversion, do pastors and churches need it? A young pastor and his wife came to our Ashram and as they drove along they reluctantly planned to separate. They could not make a go of it. At the Ashram they each surrendered the "self" to Christ. Then having surrendered to Christ they found it easy to surrender to each other. They went back "as on a honeymoon." Now they are winning others to Christ and the church is alive. They both needed conversion from their unsurrendered egos.

Will the church outgrow the necessity of producing conversion? Yes, when the eye outgrows the necessity of light, the lungs outgrow the necessity of air, the heart outgrows the necessity of love, life outgrows the necessity of life. It is a built-in necessity. I repeat the English psychiatrist's statement: "Man is made for conversion."

Will the modern age listen to the appeal for conversion? It will if those that proclaim it have it. And it will flock to the churches that illustrate it as a converted society. Paul's last recorded spoken words were these: "They will listen" (Acts 28:28 RSV). They were spoken to the Jews about the Gentiles —he said the Gentiles would listen if the Jews didn't. It was the summing-up of a life conclusion when all around him spoke the opposite. He was under Roman arrest in a foreign country, under suspicion or opposed by his countrymen, yet he spoke one of the most optimistic sentences in history: "They will listen." And the point is that it was true—the Gentiles have listened, listened as they have to no one else. The name of Jesus is not merely written into Western civilization—it is plowed in. More books have been written about Jesus than about any hundred others. And wherever they have listened, listened and obeyed, to that degree life has been ennobled, purified, and regenerated. A prisoner saw that, bet his life on it—and won. A prisoner was the freest man of his age, or of any age. And he gained his freedom through Jesus the crucified— the crucified became the most alive man in history, and made more people alive than any person who ever lived. He still does.

At the age of eighty-six I repeat Paul's words and repeat them with emphasis: "They will listen." I was to speak in a university Convocation on "Sadie Hawkins Day." The students came in rube costumes and were greeted with uproarious applause.

The more absurd the costume the more uproarious the applause. The Dean leaned over to me as we sat on the platform and whispered: "You've got your hands full this morning." When it came to my turn to speak in less than a minute there was a pin-drop silence, and at the close when I gave the invitation for personal decision for Christ, two hundred of those students responded. Down under Sadie Hawkins Day costumes was a deep yearning for reality, for God, and they responded. "They will listen."

One night I spoke in Delhi, India, and the next night in Tampere, Finland. The State Church Lutheran Bishop had asked the Dean of the cathedral, which held two or three thousand, to ask me to have an altar service at the close of the address. I wouldn't have had nerve enough to do it on my own, not in a state cathedral, but they asked for it, and did they respond? They filled the altar with two or three rows behind, and were also kneeling down the aisles. "They will listen."

I spoke to a Roman Catholic high school with 1,300 students in a Pennsylvania city on "What may a modern person believe?" At the close they gave not only the usual customary applause, they jumped to their feet and gave a standing ovation and waved their hands. "They will listen."

This age is homesick for God. It is confused and empty and can't stand the emptiness. The head of a sorority said to me: "My generation is an uncommitted generation—the next generation will be committed to a mental institution."

The emptiness of this generation is the greatest field for evangelism that we have ever faced. This emptiness is getting more empty—our opportunity for evangelism will not decrease, but increase. Buber says: "The increase of self-knowledge will lead to self-destruction or to new birth." This is a profound diagnosis: Increase in self-knowledge equals self-destruction or new birth. So self-knowledge will drive you down to self-destruction—to suicide—or will drive you up to self-consecration to God and a consequent new birth.

When we set up the Nurmanzil Psychiatric Center in Lucknow, India, the first of its kind, we defined the relationship of psychiatry carried on under Christian auspices and the Christian faith as follows: "Christian psychiatry helps the patient to become sufficiently footloose mentally and emotionally and spiritually to make an intelligent surrender to God and to contribute to the patient's techniques to cultivate that new birth consequent upon that surrender to God." The end is not to know himself, but to know God. "This is eternal life that they may know God and Jesus Christ whom thou hast sent." The end is not self-knowledge, but God-knowledge through Jesus Christ. Then, and then only, do you know yourself as a child of God and being made into the likeness of the Son of God. That knowledge does not lead to self-destruction, but to further self-consecration—to growth in that likeness of the Son of God. This gives an eternal goal and an eternal growth— the finite always approaching the Infinite but never becoming the Infinite. Those who make becoming God the goal follow a will-of-the-wisp which leads to the swamps of despair and disillusionment. One such aspirant to Messiah I interviewed many years ago in India. I said to him: "I want you to be like Christ, but to be another Christ is a tall order." He replied: "Oh, d—— it all." Later he renounced being a Messiah, saying: "I'd rather be a truck driver than be a Messiah." He was floundering in the swamps of disillusionment. A write-up of him in a modern journal was entitled, "A Philosopher of Nothing." He wanted to be everything and became "nothing."

But to be reborn is an open possibility to everybody, everywhere, in any condition, in any circumstances. That is the open door—the one universal open door—to mankind. The words of an evangelist? Then listen to Toynbee, the historian: "The necessary condition for making technology bear fruit that will be sweet and not bitter is a spiritual change of heart."

"I will give them one heart and I will put a new spirit within you, and I will take the stony heart out of their flesh and will give them a heart of flesh." This spiritual need is our crying need. Toynbee continues, "Without it our new-found virtuosity in transplanting physical organs will be of no avail and when we land deftly on the moon, the physical dust and ashes we shall find there will be an ironical reminder of our unredeemed spiritual barrenness on our mother earth."

Alongside the historian stands the medical fraternity in the person of the head of a medical college who said to me: "If you ministers can't produce conversion we doctors will have to. For our offices are filled with people passing on the sickness of their minds and souls to their bodies and they will never be well until they change their attitudes toward life." To the medical witness we add the psychiatric: Dr. Boss, perhaps the outstanding psychiatrist of Europe, wrote to me when I sent him a copy of my book on conversion: "This is the kind of a book we need—a book on 'Conversion.' Those psychiatrists who are not superficial have come to the conclusion that the vast neurotic misery of the world could be termed a neurosis of emptiness. Men cut themselves off from the root of their being, God, and then life turns meaningless, empty, and sick. Then we get them as psychiatrists."

This emptiness will not get less acute, it will get more. And it will become wider and wider in range as the undeveloped nations become more and more developed. This should not fill us with dismay, but with eager anticipation. For there is nothing, absolutely nothing, that can fill that emptiness except the unshakable Kingdom, the Kingdom of God, and the unchanging Person, the Son of God, the absolute order and the absolute person. There is nothing else on the field. The alternatives are unworkable stopgaps, temporary expedients, soporifics, crutches. There is only one cure—Jesus Christ.

This need for conversion is deeply rooted in experience and in Scripture. In the last chapter of Revelation, almost the last verse is this: " 'Come!' say the Spirit and the Bride. 'Come!' let each hearer reply. Come forward, you who are thirsty" (Rev. 22:17 NEB). (Does this "come forward" point to public decision?) "Let him who desires take the water of life without price" (Rev. 22:17 RSV). What does this amazing verse mean? Apparently this: After God has done everything as described in the whole book of Scripture there is nothing else to be done, for he has done all—nothing else, for us who follow him except to say "Come." And when we say "Come," we are not alone— two others say "Come," "the Spirit and the Bride." The Spirit says "Come" in every man. For every man is built by his very nature to receive this redemption. We are made by Christ and for Christ and when we find him we find ourselves. He is our homeland. And all coming to him has the feel of a homecoming on it. All going away from him has the feeling of estrangement upon it. When we find him we find ourselves. When we know him we know ourselves. When we live with him we can live with ourselves. And vice versa, when we won't live with him we can't live with ourselves.

So the Holy Spirit is whispering in every man: "Come." We have an ally in every man's heart who has already been saying, "Come," before we say our "Come." So the ground is laid already in every man's heart. Yours is not a strange voice when you say to him, "Come." It is the echo of the Divine Voice speaking within him. So the ground is prepared for the Good News. Man is structured for Christ, and therefore fulfilled in him. Without him—unfulfilled. Thirsty.

In his, "Hound of Heaven," Francis Thompson vividly portrays this accord between nature and grace: "All things betray thee, who betrayest Me." "All things fly thee, for thou flyest Me." Harvey Cox puts it thus: "The relationship between subjective and objective hope raise in Block's mind the question of identity between the man who hopes and the structure of reality which supports and nourishes that hope." Block is a skeptic, but he saw the identity between the God of grace and the God of nature—we are structured by him and for him.

And the "Bride" says come. The Bride is the church. Those who belong to the Bride, the invisible church, say "Come." And if they do not say "Come" they do not belong to the invisible church, even though they may belong to the visible church. So if anyone is not saying "Come," he has lost his right to be called Christian.

Now note: "Let everyone who hears say, 'Come.'" If he doesn't say "Come," he will not have anything to say "Come" to. For it is a law of the mind that that which is not expressed dies. So a Christian that is not witnessing will soon have nothing to witness to. All expression deepens impression.

A layman came to his pastor and said: "Pastor, I heard you preach on, 'Let him that heareth say *Come*. Now all my life I've been hearing, but I've never once said to anybody 'Come'; it's time for me to begin. My business is in such shape that I need give it only four hours a day. I'd like to give four hours a day to Christ and the church. Give me a job." The pastor, who was a pastor of a very large church, said, "Here is a list of the people who belong to the church but never come. See what you can do with them." He went to everyone of them, talked with them, prayed with them, loved them, and won a lot of them. Came back to the pastor and asked for another job. The pastor gave him his "prospect list," a list of people in the city who ought to be Christians but whom he had not been able to win. He went to everyone of them and won a lot of them. He went back to the pastor for another list and was given a list of the students belonging to the local university who had registered themselves as having "no religious affiliation." He was not a university man, but was so sincere, so straightforward that he won a lot of the students. By this time the pastor was running out of lists and said: "Here is a list from the Chamber of Commerce of the people who have moved into the city of Des Moines in the last two years. See what you can do with them." To make a long story short, every year for four years an average of two hundred people stood before the altars of that church to become members— eight hundred in four years. Others went into other churches. Before he began this work this man had had trouble with his heart. He had a lot of time on his hands so he was giving himself attention pains. But he forgot all about his heart in winning people and it settled down to normalcy. He couldn't make a speech, but he could love people and witness to them. He had been a dud, now he was dynamic.

As I have written previously, when a prisoner of Rome said of us: "They will listen," he uttered one of the truest words in history—and the most important. For as a result of that listening to Jesus Christ, his name has not been written into the civilization of the West, it has been watermarked into it. That name, plowed into the soul of Christendom has been, and still is, the seed of all that is fine and beautiful and progressive in our civilization. And where that name has become dim or nonexistent that civilization has decayed to the degree of that dimming. A judge puts it in this way: "Almost all juvenile delinquency comes out of non-Sunday school youth and almost all divorces come out of nonchurchgoing groups." Even where the personal contact with Jesus in Sunday school and church is dim and impersonal, it makes a difference, even at secondhand. Where it is firsthand and vital it makes all the difference in the world.

Even in other parts of the world the Gentiles have listened— listened out of necessity. For mankind is running up against the stark fact that life in general works well in a Christian way and badly in an unchristian way. In Japan, for instance, I was told by a Japanese businessman that the basic idea in Japan before the war was that "business is like a folding screen; it only stands if it is crooked." "Now," he said, "we have found that business cannot stand if it is crooked. It can only stand if it is straight, so we have adopted the mottoes of 'loving your neighbor as you love yourself' and 'doing unto others as you would have them do unto you.' " Their economy tended to break down under crookedness, but went up under the Christian basic attitudes. "They will listen"—they will have to, for you run against the grain of the universe if you act and think in an unchristian way, and you work with the grain of the universe when you think and act in a Christian way. For the universe is made in its inner structure to work in a Christian way and in no other. By trial and error we are finding that out. We are listening out of sheer necessity.

An Indian governor, though a Hindu, said to a Hindu doctor: "You are doing a real bit of Christian service in this leper colony." In the dedication of a Hindu college it was said by a speaker, a Hindu: "Let us make this a real missionary college." It ran better in a Christian way. A Hindu said to me in reference to a Moslem: "Well I hope I took a Christian attitude toward him." A Hindu taking a Christian attitude toward a Mohammedan! Mixed, but illuminating! Life worked better that way!

A Hindu doctor and a Greek masseuse, both sympathetic to Hindu thought and attitudes, visited many of the Hindu Ashrams and sacred places and came back to the Sat Tal Ashram and reported, "It is the twilight of the Gurus. The Gurus are worshiped and offered reverence, but they have no power to change the individual or society. They have no divine spark for regenerating those who come to them." They go away awed but not altered. That will be the verdict on the Christian movement if we do not "listen" to Christ in regard to evangelizing. If we do not evangelize we will evaporate. It will be the twilight of the Christian movement. We must listen and live!

God may have other words for other worlds, but for this world his word is Christ and Christ's word is, "Go forth therefore and make all nations my disciples" (Matt. 28:19 NEB). "And all the time I will be with you" (Matt. 28:20 Moffatt.)

When is the promise of being "with you" made? When you are making "all nations my disciples." At the time when you are evangelizing at home and abroad, for evangelizing one's own nation is a part of "all nations." When does he promise to be with us? If our doctrines are sound? Perhaps, but not necessarily. When our ritual is ornate and impressive? Perhaps, but not necessarily. When our preaching is eloquent? Perhaps, but not necessarily. When we are winning people to our church? Perhaps, but not necessarily. But the promise of being "with you" is specifically made when you are making disciples and note "*my* disciples." The emphasis is "my." We are to make disciples, not of us, but of Jesus Christ. Not of our system, but of him personally.

Perhaps they do not "listen" because we are presenting a system, our selves, our group, our civilization, and not him. It is one thing to be a disciple of a system, a human person, a human group, or a civilization, and quite another to be a disciple of Jesus Christ—the Divine Redeemer and Lord. There I can put my full weight down. And only there! So I have to apologize before the non-Christian world for Western civilization because it is only partly Christian; for Western forms of Christianity, because they are only partly Christian; for myself, because I am only a Christian-in-the-making, but for Jesus Christ there are no apologies on my lips for there are none in my heart. Here I have the purest and most wholesome motive for evangelization—"make all nations my disciples"—that has ever been found or can be found. For it attaches me in soul and outer allegiance to the best character that has ever appeared on this planet, without exception and without rival.

> If Jesus Christ is a man—
> And only a man,—I say
> That of all mankind I cleave to him,
> And to him will I cleave alway.

> If Jesus Christ is God—
>   And the only God,—I swear
> I will follow him through heaven and hell,
> The earth, the sea, the air! [1]

So, in the soul of the reconstructed church there must be evangelism, for evangelism is the soul of our faith.

The business of religion is to produce conversion—to make bad men into good men, weak men into strong men, selfish men into unselfish men, and unloving men into loving men. And when the church can no longer produce that miracle it has lost its right to be called Christian, for it is of the essence of being Christian to produce that miracle.

This need for conversion will persist after the ghettoes have been wiped out and poverty has been abolished. Conversion has been the greatest incentive for, and instrument in, abolishing both, when it has been real Christian conversion. But to substitute the aim of wiping out ghettoes and the wiping out of poverty for conversion is to substitute the marginal for the central. There is as much acute misery in the unconverted affluent society as there is in the unconverted poor. A very happy and useful woman who was converted in an affluent society says: "Of the circle in which I moved before conversion, two committed suicide, three ended in mental institutions, ten were divorced—only two marriages survived, mine and one other and the other is shaky." There was as much concentrated misery in that affluent group as in any other group anywhere, and real Christian conversion would have saved every person involved and every situation from decay and dissolution. For as Dr. Jung, the psychiatrist, says: "Of all the people who come to me after thirty-five years of age suffering from nervous upset and breakdown, I have found none who have come to this condition except through a loss of faith, and I have found none who have ever regained their

---

[1] Richard Watson Gilder, "The Song of a Heathen."

health except as they have regained a faith." One woman objected and said: "But Dr. Jung, you don't believe in these dogmas of the church, do you?" To which he replied: "Madam, I am not a priest, I am a doctor. All I can say is that if you gain a faith you may get well, but if you don't gain a faith you won't get well."

In Africa, where this is written, a doctor told me yesterday that nervous diseases and breakdowns are increasing alarmingly. The same phenomena is to be found in America as a doctor said to me as he pointed out the offices of General Motors: "Seventy-five percent of these young executives are suffering from stomach ulcers due to the pressure to succeed. I was trained to treat the body with physical remedies for physical diseases, so I don't know what to do with these people whose physical diseases are rooted in the mental and spiritual." A surgeon said to me: "You could have headed off 85 percent of the people who come to me for surgery by the kind of religion you are manifesting. Their need for surgery begins in functional disturbance brought on by wrong mental and spiritual attitudes. This functional disturbance passes into structural disease, then I get them as a surgeon."

So as Paul says, "They will listen." They will have to— out of necessity. This is a physically minded age. If I say: "This will hurt your soul," they will inwardly say: "So what?" But if I say: "This will give you a stomach ulcer," the reply will be: "Then I must do something about it." So physical and social and business and political necessities are combining with moral and spiritual necessities to compel men to listen.

Take business: A friend is a management engineer. When he takes hold of a business to put it on its feet again, he finds that 95 percent of difficulties are not found in the business itself but in the persons concerned. Men get snarled up with themselves, project those snarls into their situation, cooperation dies, and the business turns sick. He says he cannot straighten out that business until he straightens out the people. So he sits till midnight with executives and heads of departments and they reply to him: "Yes, we are snarled up with ourselves—we can't live with ourselves and we can't live with others. But how do you get unsnarled?" My friend has to tell them of God, a point of reference outside themselves to break the tyranny of self-interest and free them from self-preoccupation. "Yes," they say, "but how do you find God?" Then he has to tell them of conversion, of new birth. "Yes, but how do you find conversion?" He then recommends to them a book like *Abundant Living*. Now what was that group doing? Having a religious meeting? No, trying to straighten out a business and running straight into conversion—by necessity.

Take the modern vogue for analytic psychiatry. It was supposed to take the place of the necessity of religion: Analyze the patient and it will heal him. But Dr. Appleby, head of the Psycho-Analytic Society of America, said: "After reducing the patient by analysis to an anxiety of nothingness we must bring in religion to give back meaning and purpose to life." The phrase "anxiety of nothingness" is revealing. Psychoanalysis in reducing life to anxiety in general by "dissolving the basis of faith in the acids of modern thinking" has tended to produce this anxiety of nothingness. This anxiety of nothingness is at the basis of physical and social sickness, at the basis of men turning to drugs, to stimulants—anything to give a temporary lift to life. But all pick-me-ups result in a let-me-down, a vicious circle. Now drugs are being used to help people see God. I said to a holy man, a sadhu, in India, "Why do you take marijuana?" He replied: "It makes me see God." I replied: "It makes you drunk." He replied: "An ordinary man like you it makes drunk, but it makes me see God." The God that can be seen only when the brain and nerves are disordered is a God who isn't worth seeing. The God that can be seen only when one is cracked is a cracked God. Suppose we universalize that and humanity drugged itself to see a cracked God. That humanity would be a cracked humanity—subhuman. The God that I see in Christ can be seen by loving him "with all thy mind" (the intellectual nature), "with all thy heart" (the emotional nature), "with all thy soul" (the willing nature), and "with all thy strength"—the strength of the mind, the emotions, the will, the whole person. That is affirmation of the person; druggism is escapism, a failure of nerve, "crutches for lame ducks." The disillusionment that follows these adventures in unreality will compel this modern age to listen. The vogue turns to the vague and the vague to the vacuum and the vacuum compels one to turn, to listen to Christ the Real, the Realizer, the Redeemer. "All things betray thee, who betrayest Me."

Many who do not turn to the illusion of drugs and stimulants turn to rebirth, to transmigration, as a way out of their present emptiness. Rebirth is a substitute for new birth. This is an illusion. Some disciples asked Jesus concerning the man born blind: "Who did sin, this man (in his previous birth) or his parents that he was born blind?" Jesus replied, "Neither did this man sin (in a previous birth) or his parents (in a previous birth or in this one) that he was born blind, but that the works of God might be manifest in him."

A Japanese professor was blinded in mid-career by a detached retina. Being a Buddhist he went to his Buddhist scriptures and they told him that his blindness was the result of sin in a previous birth. He couldn't believe it. He came to this incident in the New Testament and heard it with surprise and hope: "Could the works of God be manifest through my blindness?" He listened to Christ, surrendered to him, and walked out of his despair. He became a flaming evangelist. Men flocked to hear a man who could turn the worst into the best. This was victory! He went to Scotland for postgraduate education, taught theology in Kobe University, wrote books, and lived radiantly—in spite of! Suppose he had turned for the answer to rebirth, sin in a previous birth. He would not know what sin it was so he could correct it. For fault and memory were not connected. What kind of a judicial system would that be that punishes or rewards with no connecting memory link? "But some do remember their previous birth" is the answer. Suppose some do, then everybody should if it is a universal law embracing everybody. Since there is no universal remembrance of a previous birth, I question those who claim they do remember. It is probably imagination, or fabrication, conscious or unconscious, to gain attention. There is absolutely no proof of it in Scripture or experience. Moreover, there is a valid and vital alternative for rebirth, and that is new birth in this birth. When one is "born from above" this is a perfect and total substitute for the necessity of a rebirth in order to get rid of one's sins and to be a different person. One no longer depends on an unprovable hypothesis of a rebirth, but he has a realized experience of a Redeemer and Savior now. Moreover, he is no longer afraid of death—"to be absent from the body is to be present with the Lord." The follower of Jesus goes from a "present with the Lord" now to a "present with the Lord" then. The necessity of rebirth is cancelled by the fact of new birth now.

If the belief in rebirth were to become dominant in a nation it would prove fatalistic and would paralyze that nation. When calamity, individual or collective, struck it, it would make that nation tap its forehead and say, "My karma is bad. I'm suffering from sin in a previous birth. I can do nothing but suffer." Whereas, if a nation believes in a new birth now, it can change and be changed and it could and would tackle its sufferings now and do away with the causes of them now. A man would not be fatalistic, but factualistic—he would face the facts and change them now. The civilization produced out of the "change-now" emphasis would be progressive and dynamic.

The disillusionment that will certainly come through following belief in rebirth will make us "listen" to Jesus. For belief in rebirth is no hopeful hypothesis, for the originators of rebirth, the Hindus, say you must go through 82,000,000 rebirths before you are released from its weary round. Could anything be more hopeless and barren? Salvation to the Hindus means salvation from rebirth. Jesus gives that now when he offers and gives new birth now. He who has new birth has no need for rebirth, for new birth is salvation now in this birth.

Again, those who have been looking to the stars, to astrology, for guidance in life will have to "listen" to Jesus when disillusionment sets in. For turning to the stars for guidance is a sign of decay. This is materialism pure and simple, matter deciding the life of moral beings! And yet we are told that five million people in the United States decide their lives by astrology. And of all silly things, the fact that newspapers of America print this horoscope business is the silliest. Following astrology is in the class of those who depended on chicken livers for guidance among the Greeks and Romans, and will bring the same decay. The devotees of astrology will "listen" to Jesus—will have to when disillusionment sets in, as it is bound to do, for stargazing for life guidance is silly, and worse, it is a blight on any civilization that adopts it.

But these things I have mentioned as leading to disillusionment are minor compared to the vast disillusionment which will come and is coming from secularism. After the wave of enthusiasm for the secular as sacred, which is sweeping some portions of the church and which will leave a deposit of the secular as an important area of evangelism, the idea will have spent itself and will leave disillusionment behind. People will then "listen" to the Gospel of the Kingdom of God. For the Gospel of the Kingdom of God gives the real relationship between the secular and the sacred.

In two places in the Acts of the Apostles the message of evangelism, the Good News, is given by two evangelists, the most successful of those early days. Philip and Paul defined that Gospel as: "But when they believed Philip, who preached the gospel of the reign of God and the name of Jesus, they had themselves baptized" (Acts 8:12 Moffatt). This from Philip the layman. And this from the apostle Paul at the very mature end of his career when he spoke to the Jews who came to him while he was in his house imprisonment at Rome: "From morning to evening he explained the Reign of God to them from personal testimony, and tried to convince them about Jesus" (Acts 28:23 Moffatt) and then: "For two full years he remained in his private lodging, welcoming anyone who came to visit him; he preached the Kingdom of God and taught about the Lord Jesus Christ quite openly and unmolested" (Acts 28:30-31 Moffatt). In both places the gospel was defined as the kingdom of God and the person of Jesus Christ —the absolute order and the absolute person.

The kingdom of God, the absolute order, is to operate in the secular—"Thy kingdom come and thy will be done on earth as it is in heaven." Its sphere is "on earth" in the sphere of the secular, but the Kingdom is not the secular, and the secular is not the Kingdom. The secular is the relative and the Kingdom is the absolute. The secular becomes the sacred when, and only when, it is dedicated to the Kingdom. When it is dedicated to itself it is secular and only secular, earthbound and material-bound. The secular gets its meaning by being dedicated to something other than itself and higher than itself, the moral and spiritual, to God and his Kingdom. When the secular tries to be an end in itself by saying that the secular is the sacred, then it is idolatry; for when a relative thing claims to be an absolute thing that is idolatry pure and simple. In the old paganism an idol, a physical idol, was invested with sacred qualities—was God. That paganism is passing away. But now a new and all-embracing paganism is being insisted upon, namely, an all-embracing idolatry in that the material universe is sacred and therefore God. This is the vastest and the most egotistical claim that the secular is sacred ever imagined by man; man and his civilization, and the earth on which that civilization is founded, become sacred and therefore become

God. "Seek first the secular and all these things shall be added unto you" is its claim, and its slogan, and its sin, the sin of substituting man and his works for God.

If man and his works are dedicated to the truly sacred, the kingdom of God and the command of Jesus is given as its central aim: "Seek first the kingdom of God and his righteousness and all these things (the secular) will be added to you," then everything falls into its proper place. The kingdom of God is the supreme loyalty. If man and the secular are subordinated to and loyal to that Kingdom, then all these things (the secular) will be added. Otherwise they will be subtracted, even if added to, for their very abundance will be a burden. The affluent society becomes the burdened society, disillusioned and fed up and empty. It has everything—and nothing. A woman said to me: "I don't have to work, I have money, but I work to keep from committing suicide. My husband doesn't have to work, he has money, but he works to run away from himself."

As sure as fate, in the present generation and succeeding generations, if they make the material an end in itself instead of a "means" to the ends of the Kingdom of God, a vast disillusionment will set in. A pastor in England preached a sermon on a caterpillar which climbed a green painted stick in search of green leaves but got to the top of the barren stick and had to climb down again, disillusioned. A millionaire heard the sermon and wrote the pastor; "Have you got anything to offer to a tired millionaire? I have climbed to the top of that green painted stick of making money, have got to the top, and will have to climb down again to find how to live. I'm empty."

A disillusioned age will "listen," will have to. Lin Yutang, a Chinese writer, was a Christian who gave it up and became a secularist, who glorified secularism in his writings. But he became disillusioned, found it shallow, found that man could "not live by bread alone." He came back to Christ and wrote a book about his return entitled, *From Pagan to Christian,* ending a chapter in these words: "Put out the candles, the sun is up." Put out the candles, the half answers, the Sun is up. Jesus Christ is alive and available and his answer answers, totally and satisfactorily for life. A white woman in Rhodesia who had lost her faith in secularism said, "When I read those words, 'Put out the candles, the sun is up,' I surrendered myself to Christ and for me the Sun was up." That will be increasingly the mood of civilization around the world, including communism. For communism as a military and political power is still strong, but as a gospel of liberation to suppressed people it has lost or is losing its appeal. I said that in the presence of a former president of India, Dr. Rajendra Parshad, and he struck the table with his fist and said: "I entirely agree." I write this in Nairobi, Africa. Out of the fifty new nations set up in Africa not one has become Communist; some have become leftist, but not Communist.

All these I have mentioned are roads with dead ends. Those that take them will have to back out in disappointment and disillusionment. Then they will back into the kingdom of God out of necessity. No other way opens out of futility.

Is this what all these modern revolts are seeking for—the Kingdom of God—and don't know it? Yes. The central characteristic of modern revolts is that they are revolting against something, but they do not know what they are revolting for? They are revolting against the status quo, but they are confused, dreadfully confused, as to what they are revolting for. We believe they are revolting for the Kingdom of God. They are revolting unconsciously for that Kingdom, and don't know it. And this includes the central revolt, communism.

A Communist said to Dr. MacLeod of Scotland, "Dr. MacLeod, do you know you Christians have got the answer, if you only knew it, and if you knew how to say it." Twenty out of the one hundred members of our Sat Tal Ashram in India were once members of the Communist Party. One announced at the first meal that he was a Communist. We didn't explode or segregate him, but treated him like the rest and gave him a job. The last day he said:

Brother Stanley, will you please pray for me. I want to become a Christian again. When I was a member of the Communist Party in the university, two members of the Party—not one but two, for they couldn't trust one—came to check up on me every day. I came here and announced that I was a Communist and you gave me a job and never came to check up on me, and treated me as a person. I want to get back into a society of trust from a society of suspicion.

He became the auditor of a Christian mission.

When Thomas Edison told that he had made 1,100 experiments, all of which had turned out failures, someone said to him: "Then you've wasted your time." "No," replied Dr. Edison, "I found out 1,100 ways how not to do things." Today men everywhere are finding out how not to do things, how not to live. And they are getting hurt in the process. The biggest hurt is inner disillusionment and cynicism ending in bitterness and negativism and revolt. But men cannot live on a No, for they are not negative beings. They are positive and must live by the positive, and Jesus is that Great Positive. Listen to these words: "The divine 'yes' has at last sounded in him, for in him is the 'yes' that affirms all the promises of God" (II Cor. 1:19-20 Moffatt) .

When this prodigal generation living in a far country, an alien land, and living on the husks of negativisms gets tired of the emaciating diet, it will come back to the Father's house, the Kingdom of God, and will begin to live by the divine 'yes' it will know that this is the Homeland. Sheer necessity will drive it to that Homeland. Mankind is sick—with homesickness.

So the word of the Spirit to us moderns as we worship is the same as the word of the Spirit in that day: "Evangelize."

For conversion is as necessary in the affluent society as it is in the poverty-stricken society. For the affluent are often affluent outwardly and poverty-stricken within. Whatever the outward condition of man he still needs conversion. So conversion is a built-in necessity, not something imposed.

The reconstructed church must specialize in conversion, for that is its special business. It is the one movement dedicated to character change. All other movements specialize in the minor—the training of the mind, the emotions, the adornment of the body, the health of the body, the environmental world, physical food. But one movement, the church, is dedicated to character change in the individual and in society. And that is major.

What do I mean by conversion? The best definition of conversion is found in a converted person. This is written in the heart of Africa, in Zambia. Festo Kodagre was a typical, well-educated, modern young man. He says he was a drunkard. The Uganda revival was on. Teen-age girls arose at the close of an Anglican service and quoted: "Come unto me all ye that labor and are heavy laden and I will give you rest." Another rose and gave her interpretation from experience. The congregation was spellbound at this spontaneity amid Anglican conformity. Another teacher was converted and went to Festo three hours after his conversion to set things right with him. Festo was so moved that he went on to his knees and was converted. Seeing a woman going by he called out: "Jesus has come to me." The woman, knowing him, thought he was mocking and told a group so. But Festo himself came to the group and they saw at a glance that his conversion was real. Two teen-age nieces, who had been praying for him and had said to him that he would be converted that week, ran and threw their arms around his neck and wept. The group gathered around him and sang and rejoiced. A big African picked him up and marched around with Festo on his shoulders, saying he was the shepherd who had found his "one lost sheep." The group stayed at Festo's house all night rejoicing. It was a return of the prodigal. Festo has won thousands upon thousands to Christ, and he was won by a man who had only been in the Kingdom three hours! The revival has been going for forty years unabated. Still going on! And it was started by two laymen, one an English medical doctor, Dr. Church, and the other a converted government official, an African.

A dean of a theological seminary in America came to Africa, as he puts it, "an evangelical liberal and went back to America a liberal evangelical." Everyone needs conversion, from the dean of a theological seminary to an alcoholic African and all types between. Man as man needs conversion.

Conclusion Number Eleven: God is saying to this age what he has said to every age, and will say to the ages to come: "Except ye be converted and become as little children ye shall not enter the kingdom of God," and "Except a man be born again he cannot see the Kingdom of God." Conversion and new birth are the deepest needs of this age or any age, for the intelligence of man has outrun his capacity to handle that intelligence. We have more power than we can safely handle. Every generation needs regeneration—this one especially.

XIII

WHAT DOES ANTIOCH CONTRIBUTE TO THE MODERN CHURCH?

First, a new beginning was made in a new matrix. As *The Interpreter's Bible* puts it: "The swaddling clothes were at last completely stripped off." [1] The headquarters of the church was changed from Jerusalem to Antioch. The hierarchal system with its so-called apostolic succession centered in Jerusalem. This goes back to the apostles. But the movement in Antioch goes back to Christ—they were Christ-ians. The future belonged to Christ and the people. "There has never been a better name by which to describe the followers of Christ. We are not Catholic or Protestant, liberals or orthodox. We are Christians." [2] Our unity is to be found in Christ. One denomination has taken the name "The Christian Church," also "The Disciples." Let them keep the name of "The Disciples" and leave the name "Christian" to all of us.

Second, it was a lay church, founded by laymen and animated and carried on by laymen. The center of gravity of that church was the laity. The full-time workers in the Christian movement, Paul and Barnabas, were "guests of the church" (Acts 11:26 RSV), or as the New English Bible puts it, they "lived in fellowship with the congregation there." They were not

[1] IX (Nashville: Abingdon Press, 1954), p. 146b.
[2] *Ibid.*, p. 149-50b.

overlords of the local church, they did not run the church, they were "guests," "in fellowship with the congregation." This fits in with the declared aim and end of the various "gifts": "and these were his gifts: some to be apostles, some prophets, some evangelists, some pastors and teachers, to equip God's people for work in his service" (Eph. 4:12 NEB). Note that the work of the apostles, prophets, evangelists, pastors, and teachers is *"to equip God's people for work in his service."* It was not for God's people, the laity, to look on and listen while the apostles, prophets, evangelists, pastors, and the teachers performed. All of these were for one thing. And who were the laity? The word for laity comes from the Greek *laos* and it means "the people of God."

A Roman Catholic priest was asked, "What is the church?" and he replied: "The people of God." "Not the hierarchy?" "No, the people of God." Then the hierarchy is not the end, to be bowed down to and to be obeyed by the people of God. The whole of the hierarchy is for one thing and one thing alone: "to equip God's people" for the work of the ministry. Not for subordinate service, taking collections and ushering and setting up the stage for the ministers to perform, but for the work of the ministry—the laity were the ministers. The King James Version puts it: "for the perfecting of the saints, for the work of the ministry." The laity were to be trained for "the work of the ministry," not odd jobs.

This puts the laity at the center and not in the margin. The chief business of the paid ministry is to be the guides, stimulators, and spiritualizers of an essentially lay movement. This would vitalize the paid ministry and be according to New Testament pattern and meet present-day needs. For lay witnessing is the key to the future.

This leaves the possibility of bishops functioning in the church, provided they are chosen by the laity and the paid ministry, as those who would be the coaches of the coaches.

Third, it gives the pattern of a church that cares—at two

levels, the economic and the evangelistic, the moral and spiritual. The church at Antioch sent a relief expedition to Jerusalem when a famine was on—by the hands of Paul and Barnabas. And they sent an evangelistic expedition into Asia and Europe by the same Paul and Barnabas. They cared about the economic need, and they cared about the moral and spiritual need. These two things were the alternate beats of the Christian heart.

Today there is a pressure on the churches to emphasize the material; poverty is the chief evil, and the ghetto the chief object, of renewal. This is a bird trying to fly with one wing— it goes around in circles. The Christian movement includes in its program five items:

The Spirit of the Lord is upon me, because he hath annointed me to preach the gospel to the poor (the economically disinherited) ; . . . to preach deliverance to the captives [the socially and politically disinherited], and recovering of sight to the blind [the physically disinherited], to set at liberty [according to the Aramaic, "to strengthen with forgiveness"] them that are bruised [the morally and spiritually disinherited], to proclaim the Lord's year of Jubilee.

If that be the proper translation it refers back to the Jewish Year of Jubilee, when every fifty years all debts were cancelled, all slaves freed, and all land redistributed, and the nation began to develop a closer approximation to equality. Jesus enlarged this into "the Lord's Year of Jubilee." Here the economic, the social and political, the physical, the moral and spiritual, and the collective were to be redeemed—the whole of life.

Antioch branched out in three directions: They sent relief to famine-stricken people—"everyone," note the "everyone," "gave according to his ability." Then the church won people around them at their home base, "the strong hand of the Lord was with them and a great number that believed were added to the Lord." They won people in their immediate circumstances. They were not like the lamppost that shines afar but is dark around its own base. And then they reached into Asia and Europe by sending forth Barnabas and Paul on their great missionary and evangelistic journeys. They were a church that cared—cared for the economically stricken, and the morally and spiritually stricken around them, and for other races and nations at far distances. It was a church that cared with an unlimited caring. And that caring had content; they introduced into that pagan civilization that had lost its nerve the greatest life-giving, character-changing, and hope-bringing movement that ever struck it. Dean Church, a historian, says about it: "A solemn joy went through that ancient world. Sin and evil had met their match. Men, not here and there, but on a wide scale could attain to that hitherto impossible thing for the multitudes, goodness."

That ancient world needed to be made different. And it was made different to the degree that it obeyed him. And to that degree it went up. And it still goes up to the degree that it obeys him. A civilization that was getting its guidance through chicken livers and the stars began to get its guidance through the crucified and risen Redeemer, and it began to be resurrected. Compared to the invasion of Asia and Europe by Paul and Barnabas, the conquests of the Caesars and Alexander were minor and inconsequential happenings. For these Christians introduced the leaven of a new faith and a new way of life into a decaying and groping world. They still do!

Antioch was a church that cared in regard to the economic needs, the immediate spiritual needs, and the long-range spiritual needs of a pagan world. It was a church that cared.

Fourth, the church at Antioch produced a classless society; it was not a religious class club. It held within it Manean, a foster brother of Herod, the king, and Simeon called Niger, the Black, probably a member of a lower class, and held them both as brothers "for whom Christ died." Class was eliminated.

I went out to India sixty-two years ago. Upon my arrival at

Bombay, a British woman said to me: "I'm glad to get off this boat. There are nothing but working people on it." But the "working people," the Labour Party, gave freedom to India, and her world of class snobbery collapsed before the rising tide of the people. In the book of Revelation it says: "I saw thrones, and people sat upon them." In the end the people will rule—"people sat upon the thrones." And if the church of the future is to guide the development of humanity it must be a church of the people, where "the greatest of all is the servant of all." A new greatness emerges, the servants of all. The catch is in the word "all." To be a servant of some—my race, my class, my set—does not make you great, except a great snob. One class and one class only will rule the future, the servants of all. And when they become great by service to all, then "class" will be dissolved in a brotherhood of equals, with the servants of all moving to the top in leadership through service to all.

Fifth, the church at Antioch can guide the reconstructed church in regard to its attitude toward race. Remember that the pious Jew of Jesus' day thanked God every day that he "was not born a leper, a woman, or a Gentile." In that racial climate the Antiochan church made Simeon called Niger a prophet or a teacher who laid the hands of a black man on Barnabas and Paul to commission them to preach the Gospel to Asia and white Europe. And they did it without comment as though it was the normal Christian attitude. It was. The present-day attitudes on race are subnormal and sub-Christian and anti-Christian. Jesus said to the Jewish authorities about their temple: "Behold your house is left unto you—desolate." Note the "desolate." He is saying to segregated churches: "Behold your houses are left unto you—desolate." That is his sad obituary written with tears.

There is a secular factory, Western Electric, in Shreveport, Louisiana, which occupies twenty-three acres and turns out ten thousand telephones a day with assembly lines of white and black working side by side harmoniously, getting the same wages. The room where applicants for jobs in that factory are seated is occupied equally by both races. Christ would write on that plant: "A house of prayer and production for all nations." The manager is a devoted Christian and is the word become flesh applied to very modern industry. When I asked him how he kept the factory so spotlessly clean he replied: "When I see a piece of paper lying on the floor I pick it up." So the employees do the same.

I said in my farewell address, spoken to the fifteen hundred people in the church and broadcast by TV and radio, that the most important thing I saw in Shreveport was the manufacturing plant. It was a pilot plant for the whole of the Southland and had pointed the way out of the clash of races into a brotherhood, a brotherhood where it counts, in industry.

Sixth, the reconstructed church, if it is after the pattern of Antioch, after the pattern of being Christian, will hold together strong men who differ on various issues. This is necessary, for the Christian faith produces strong men with strong views; that faith awakens the total personality and develops it physically, mentally, socially, and spiritually. Differing views will arise producing wide gaps unless there is a strong and magnetic center which holds men together in spite of differences. What is that center? Class, age, denomination, race, doctrine? They are all divisive. If I should say to any group, "What do you believe?" that group will go apart, no two believing exactly the same. But if I say, "Who do you trust?" that group will come together, one name upon their lips, one loyalty in their hearts—Jesus Christ. The "whats" divide us, the "Who" unites us. The church of the future must be united around Christ. It must be united around a simple but profound formula: "If you belong to Christ and I belong to Christ, we belong to each other." This is a fact. Everybody who belongs to Christ belongs to everyone else who belongs to Christ. "All coheres in him." (Col. 1:17 Moffatt.)

If the objection is raised that our views of Jesus Christ differ, therefore we cannot be one in him, we answer that if the center is Jesus Christ, we have only one center; we begin *with* him, whatever we may believe *about* him. Believing in him and centering around him we are exposed to him and the tendency is to have our views of him heightened. He is self-verifying. No one can be in close fellowship with him and hold small views of him. Propinquity produces propensity, nearness produces dearness. If Jesus is the center of our faith he will be the center of our affections! He was the Son of man and the Son of God. Some of us approach Jesus by way of his manhood and some by way of his Godhood, and some by both. But however we approach, we come to him and in him "all things cohere," hold together. He is the magnet which holds the scattered pieces of iron together. He is centripetal, not centrifugal. So "John Mark" issues don't divide us, they pull us together, as common danger does to chicks, making them run together under the hen, and draw closer to her and closer to each other. A Christ-centric church is a Christian-centric church—the divided spokes at the rim become one in the hub.

A denomination-centered church tends to emphasize its differences and its peculiarities. A Christ-centered church can afford to differ at the margin since it is united at the center. With one point of the compass centered in Jesus, it can let the other point sweep as far as it can go and sweep in the lesser truths centered in denominational emphases. But those who are living on denominational truths are often afraid to open their minds and hearts to other truths lest they push out or dim their own. The Christ-centered have no such fears. Only Christ is the truth. The Christ-centered church will gather together the truths in denominationalism and go beyond them —to Christ. There we know the truth and the truth makes us free, free to accept lesser truths wherever found.

Seventh, the reconstructed church will develop its leaders

and make them grow. Barnabas and Paul "taught considerable numbers" at Antioch, but Antioch also taught Barnabas and Paul. The congregation made their leaders and made them into their own likeness. They made Barnabas and Paul more "Christian."

When Barnabas came and "saw the grace of God he rejoiced." He rejoiced in other people's work. He did not find flaws in what was happening in order to make room for himself. The church was so sound and spiritually alive that it toned up Barnabas to come in contact with it. Blessed is the church which makes its pastor stay on tiptoe to keep up with them. If the church leaders helped make the church, the church helped make its pastors. It was the church fasting and praying and listening that heard the voice of God saying, "Separate me Barnabas and Saul for the work to which I have called them." It was the church pushing out its leaders rather than being prodded by its leaders. This reverses the usual process in the present-day church—the pastors are prodding the people into action and sensitivity. Here a church as a church began the greatest movement that ever invaded our planet, the Christian missionary movement.

Now remember it was the church as a church that started its leaders, Paul and Barnabas, on the moral and spiritual invasion into Asia and Europe and hence to the rest of the world! The miracle of a congregation prodding its leaders into world mission!

And moreover, it was the church that rescued the world leader from a possible eddy of seclusion at Tarsus and put him into the stream of world movements. It was after Antioch that Saul became Paul. He might have been a lost leader, lost to meditation and ingrown concern at Tarsus. How long he was in Arabia, possibly in meditation and prayer, we do not know. But the silence about Arabia is revealing, revealing a tendency to long withdrawal. But Antioch saved a leader to his task of the long road and made him a world evangelist. The church held a crown above the heads of their leaders and watched them grow up into it. The crowning act was to set them apart for world evangelism! The church would run their own affairs and keep the home fires going while they were gone!

Eighth, the reconstructed church must be a church that does not bear oppositions but uses them. The Tamils of South India have a proverb: "He who has been born in the fire will not fade in the sun." The Antioch church was born in the fire of Stephen's martyrdom and in the persecution that followed, so it would not fade in the sun of ordinary oppositions. But while the church at Antioch was quiet after the stormy beginnings in its founding, this church became the storm center of the world. This quiet in Antioch was like the quiet at the center of a cyclone. That quiet center is where the forces of the cyclone reside. The church at Antioch had a quiet dynamic center but it was sending out forces that were shaking the world. "These people who have turned the world upside down have come hither also," said the people who were shaken by it. Three seismic waves went out of Antioch in the successive missionary journeys of Paul.

The church of the future must be a holy quiet where we listen to God and get his marching orders. If it is not a dynamic center, it is a dying center, the quiet of a graveyard! The question at the end of a Sunday service should be, "Not how many people gathered?" but "How many were sent out from that gathering to shake the world?" We must not merely use our oppositions, but also use our opportunities. The church at Antioch could have settled down after the storm of persecution and rejoiced in the holy quiet of worship. That would have been its decay and its doom. And yet many a Sunday morning prayer in an American church goes something like this: "We thank thee, Father, for our country, where we can worship thee without molestation, and in peace." That may be the church's obituary! This was the church's resurrection: "While they were keeping a fast and offering worship to the Lord, the Holy Spirit said: 'Set Barnabas and Saul apart for me, to do the work to which I have called them.'" The quiet turned to conquest and the conquest turned to redemption, and the redemption turned to a changed world. We of the West sit in our churches in quiet worship because Antioch listened to God in their worship and obeyed the voice that spoke.

Suppose this would be the pattern for the churches of America and the world: While the church at ——— was keeping fast and offering worship to the Lord, the Holy Spirit said, "Set ——— apart for me to do the work to which I have called them, namely, to go into full-time work in the ministry, or to the mission field, or to work for the abolition of the nearest ghetto and to give them Christ," or "to call on the unchurched and the unconverted two by two to witness and to lead them to Christ"; or "to call on the sick in hospitals and homes"; or "to identify themselves with the problems of youth and to lead them into new ways"; or "to set up employment centers for the unemployed"; or "to call on church members who never attend church and to get them to surrender to Christ and reenter the fellowship"; or "to reconcile upset families"; or "to abolish segregation of any class or race from the local Christian fellowship and membership"; or "to organize the privileged suburban community for service in the underprivileged sections"; or "to organize and promote groups for prayer and fellowship and to cultivate the spiritual life of the individuals and to uphold in prayer the pastor and those who have listened to the call of the Spirit for special service"; or "to organize recreation for those denied other opportunities for it"; or "to organize groups of men who will turn the secular into the sacred by dedicating their business, or profession, or labor to being made into opportunities to personally witness for Christ and to show by the setup and spirit and dedication that the business or profession or labor belongs to God"; or "to set up women's groups, that will be the caring edge of society, and will show that spirit of caring in everything that concerns women and children and the home"; or "to form Bible classes for study of the Word in homes, schools, offices, churches; and to form special Bible study groups for special classes such as doctors, lawyers, businessmen, and employees." And finally, "to get the church individually and collectively to surrender itself to God—a once-and-for-all surrender and a day-by-day surrender of the individual and corporate self." Then when the self is no longer on the throne, but the church has its sleeves rolled up and is ready for anything, anywhere, at any place, provided it is for him—then and then only, "the servant of all will be the greatest of all."

And note: "Set Barnabas and Saul apart *for me.*" Note that it is "for me"—these various things are done primarily for Jesus Christ, secondarily for people and causes. Making the primary motive and allegiance for Christ will hold one steady when men and situations let one down. He never does. A merely humanistic motive wears thin when people are ungrateful and disappointing. "For his sake" never grows thin, for his love never grows thin. If *they* are not grateful, *he* is! So success or failure is marginal; to be true to his "call" is central and all that matters. So the church that does these things "for me" is relieved of the inner tension of success and failure and is poised and assured and confident.

For the church that "listens to the Spirit" and "is led by the Spirit" is a Spirit-empowered church. It does things it seemingly cannot do. It is a surprise to itself and others, for it is accomplishing things beyond its powers. It is alive—with God. If the church listens to God it will be listened to by men.

But while the sending forth of Paul and Barnabas was dramatic and world-shaking, there was also a world-shaking event wrapped up in a commonplace action. It was this: "Now those who had been scattered by the trouble which arose over Stephen made their way as far as Phoenicia and Cyprus and Antioch, but they preached the word to none except Jews." They were products of Jerusalem, a racism runs through the account. But here was the breakthrough: "Some of them, however, were Cypriotes and Cyrenians, who on reaching Antioch told the Greeks also the gospel of the Lord Jesus." Had they been from Jerusalem they would have been inhibited by the Jerusalem racism. But fortunately they were from Cyprus and Cyrene and not infected by Jerusalem and so out of their Christian instincts they preached to the Greeks also. That was important. "The strong hand of the Lord was with them, and a large number believed and turned to the Lord." (Acts 11:19-21 Moffatt.) God showed his approval of this breakthrough by putting his strong hand upon them so that "a large number believed and turned to the Lord." That happened as a result of their Christian feeling that this Gospel belonged to everyone. That was the highest kind of guidance. They said, in essence, "Our Christian love and loyalty make us share this with everybody apart from racial taboos and barriers." Had that not happened Antioch would have been a Jewish racial church and therefore no pattern for a world church. They would never have been called "Christians," but Jewish believers, and I could never have written this book. For no church can be called "Christian" that is confined to one race.

We owe our Christian universality to some unknown Cypriotes and Cyreneans—the one from a small island, the other from North Africa—who without the apostles' permission or direction just did what their Christian beliefs urged them to do! They blundered into universality! It took a miracle to change Peter's idea of race, a sheet let down and a voice from God. Peter reluctantly and hesitatingly obeyed. He began to preach his gospel to the group in the house of Cornelius, Gentiles, and went beyond his own attitudes when he used the word "everyone." When he used that word God took him at his word, "and while Peter was still speaking the Holy Spirit fell upon all who listened." He was converted, but not fully, for his racial attitudes showed themselves when he refused to eat with the Gentiles when the Jews from Jerusalem were present! But these Jewish believers from Cyprus and Cyrene were just Christians, and without hesitation or delay they preached the Gospel to Greeks also. Note: "on reaching Antioch told the Greeks"—no battle with themselves and no hesitation about what the others thought. They were spontaneously Christians—a universal Christianity was the result!

Kerwin Quimagh has collected a galaxy of inspired amateurs: Herschel was a musician who became one of the greatest astronomers. Grote was a banker who became the historian of Greece. Priestly was a preacher who discovered oxygen. Schliemann was a merchant who excavated Troy. Spinoza was a grinder of lenses who took a high place among the philosophers.[3] But of all the inspired amateurs these Cypriot and Cyreanean amateurs went past the experts at Jerusalem and were the first to break the Jewish mold and universalize the Gospel as a common Christian attitude and practice. They fixed it and founded a church on it, the first church to be called "Christian." It was the lay founders of the church who set the tone of the church and made it so Christian that the only name that would describe it would be "Christian." It wasn't a name plastered on them, it was a name projected from them.

Conclusion Number Twelve: The contribution that we draw from this chapter is that Antioch produced laymen whose supreme leadership was in evangelism. There is no sign or intimation that there was an inner struggle for position and power and control of the organization. Its control and output was in evangelism. When they opened the gates for evangelism they were fulfilled. That was what they wanted and that is what they gave. All the organization was pointed toward one thing —evangelism. This was primary and all else was secondary.

---

[3] Halford Edward Luccock, *Acts of the Apostles* (Chicago: Willet, 1942), p. 52.

XIV

THE LAST AND SUPREME CONTRIBUTION

In Chapter XIII we discussed eight contributions Antioch had to offer the modern church. The ninth and supreme contribution of Antioch to the modern church demands a separate chapter.

Ninth, the church at Antioch was founded on "the Good News of the Lord Jesus." The whole passage reads:

Meanwhile those who had been scattered after the persecution that arose over Stephen made their way to Phoenicia, Cyprus, and Antioch, bringing the message to Jews only and to no others. But there were some natives of Cyprus and Cyrene among them, and these, when they arrived at Antioch, began to speak to Gentiles as well, telling them the good news of the Lord Jesus. The power of the Lord was with them, and a great many became believers, and turned to the Lord." (Acts 11:19-21 NEB.)

Note that "the power of the Lord was with them," or as Moffatt puts it, "the strong hand of the Lord was with them." It was a church which the Lord Jesus used: "And a great many became believers and turned to the Lord." It was not working with mere human energy. It was working effortlessly with the power of the Lord working through them. God was heightening

175

all their powers and they were winning Greeks and Jews and molding them into a living fellowship of the Spirit, so much so that these recent converts became the church that listened to God and heard the voice of the Spirit say: "Set apart Barnabas and Saul for me for the work I have for them." In other words, they won converts who won converts through Asia and Europe. This power was not pumped up through human organization. It was poured down into human receptivity.

The church at Antioch was founded on "the good news of Jesus Christ," the basic message of the church. "But there were some natives of Cyprus and Cyrene among them, and these when they arrived at Antioch, began to speak to pagans as well, telling them the good news of Jesus Christ." Note, not good views about Jesus Christ, but "the good news of Jesus Christ." The Gospel lies in his person. He did not come to bring the good news, he was the Good News. He did not show the way, he was the Way. He did not point to the truth, he was the Truth. He did not tell about the life, he was the Life. He knew no more sacred task than to point to his own person. Moses pointed to the Law; Mohammed to the Koran; Confucius to the Analects; Buddha to the Noble Eightfold Path. Only Jesus pointed to himself: "Come unto me." No one less than divine dare do that without blasphemy. Here infinite authority or finite audacity speaks. There can be no halfway. He is manifesting God or he is not manifesting good. And yet when we think of goodness we do not add virtue to virtue, but think of Jesus of Nazareth.

Take the fiercest revolt against Jesus Christ in recent centuries, the revolt of Nietzsche. He says: "The superman uses the 'good,' 'the beautiful' and 'the true' to affirm and promote its own life and the lives of those who are like it, to wit, the will to power." Here is the will to power by self-assertion, the ego is supreme. Alongside of that put this: "He that would be greatest among you let him be the servant of all." Put these two outlooks in life and what do they produce? One produced a Hitler and a world in ruins. The other, wherever obeyed, is producing a world in regeneration. One died in a madhouse and the other died on a cross, for others. And is alive forever more! Nietzsche and his attitudes stink in the nostrils of humanity. The superman became the subman. He broke himself on a law of the Kingdom. Nietzsche was searching for a "yes" and missed it in the crucified and risen Redeemer, for "the divine 'yes' has at last sounded in him, for in him is the 'yes' that affirms all the promises of God" (2 Cor. 1:20 Moffatt).

Nietzsche was the forerunner of those who have been seeking the divine yes—and missed it. After a long series of philosophical and religious "nos" in history, at last the "divine yes" has sounded, not in a verbal "yes" but in a vital "yes." The word "yes" became flesh in Jesus. The religions of India have been, for the most part, world weary and personality weary. The world is *maya,* an illusion. Buddha came to the conclusion that existence and suffering are one. Cut the root of desire, even for life, and you go out into that passionless, actionless state called nirvana, the state literally of "the snuffed-out candle." "Is there any existence in nirvana?" I asked a Buddhist monk in Ceylon. "How can there be?" he replied. "There is no suffering hence no existence." Buddha would get rid of the problems of life by getting rid of life. He would get rid of our headaches by getting rid of our heads. It was a vast "no." Against this background of "no" sounds not a human "yes," which might be humanistic wishful thinking, but a divine yes—Jesus Christ himself is that divine yes. All the promises of God are affirmed in him—in his very person. He didn't give a "yes"—he was the "yes."

He "affirmed the promise" that there ought to be one God, our Heavenly Father. Men have felt after the possibility of there being one God for all men who would be the Father of all men. But it was a groping. Then one day a disciple asked him: "Lord, show us the Father and it sufficeth us." And the divine "yes" sounded clear: "He that hath seen me, hath seen the Father." We gasp in surprise: "Is God a Christlike God—like Jesus in character?" If so, he is a good God and trustworthy. I could ask nothing higher; I could be content with nothing less. If God isn't like Jesus in character I have no interest in him, for "Christlike" is the highest adjective descriptive of character, in God or man, in any language. If you see God in the face of Jesus Christ, you see the real God, the lovable God, the redemptive God. When you see God somewhere else, other than in the face of Jesus Christ, you see something other than God—a figment of man's imagination instead of the figure of the God—man's revelation, our Heavenly Father. Apart from Jesus Christ we know little about God and what we know is wrong. For Jesus is "the express image of God." So apart from Jesus we go from "the new theology" to "the newer theology," to the "newest Theology." Since 1960, a book has been printed every other year and called "new theology"; the latest is called *New Theology No. 6.* They change as rapidly as women's clothes and are discarded as rapidly. Why? They have lost Jesus as the center and starting point for theology. This is obvious from the statement in *No. 4, "For theologians in the stricter sense of the term, it means that they must speak of 'the problem of God.'"* Is God a "problem"? Not if you look at him in the face of Jesus Christ. "He is altogether lovely," altogether loving, and altogether love, redeeming love. What more can we want, or ask, or need? If we are dissatisfied with the God we see in the face of Jesus Christ, then the dissatisfaction is in us, we are the problem. If we don't like the God we see in the face of Jesus Christ, it is because he doesn't like us—loves us, but doesn't like us. We are the problem.

The futility of theology without beginning with Jesus is seen in this sentence from "No. 4": *"The longer Christian past fared the fate of the recent past: iconoclasts questioned all the historic modes of theological speaking and—in the end—*

questioned the subject of theology itself." The snake in its fury swallowed itself!

The theology that begins anywhere and everywhere except Jesus Christ goes everywhere and gets nowhere. If you lose Jesus, you lose both Jesus and God. The result is a barren humanism.

Here is an outline of a theology written two thousand years ago and it is as fresh and vital and valid for today as if it were written for today, or for the next century—it is universal and timeless: "When in former times God spoke to our forefathers, he spoke in fragmentary and varied fashion through the prophets. But in this final age he has spoken to us in the Son" (Heb. 1:1-2 NEB).

Here this Hebrew writer said that revelation was progressive culminating "in the Son." He spoke *"through* the prophets in a fragmentary and varied way"—they brought a message but they were not the message and, since it came through that imperfect medium, it partook of that imperfection. So the Old Testament is pre-Christian and sub-Christian. Revelation, ultimate and final, came when God spoke *"in* the Son." The prophets were "through," the ultimate and final revelation was "in the Son." He was the message. The Gospel lies in his person. He was the Good News. All else is good views. All else is a "Tower of Babel" humanism trying to reach up to God that all ends in a confusion of tongues and futility. Religions are man's search for God, therefore there are many religions, but the Gospel is God's search for men, therefore there is but one Gospel, and that Gospel is "in the Son." We don't begin with God, for if we begin with God we begin with our ideas of God which are not God. We don't begin with man, for if we begin with man we begin with his problems, and if you begin with a problem you will probably end with a problem and, in the process will probably become a problem. We don't begin with God and we don't begin with man—

we begin with the God-Man. From him we work out to God and from him we work down to man. In his light we see life.

Christianity has its creeds, but it is not a creed; it has its doctrines, but it is not a doctrine; it has its rites and ceremonies, but it is not a rite or ceremony; it has its institutions, but it is not an institution. At its center, it is a person. Christianity is Christ.

The church at Antioch began with "the good news of Jesus Christ," "the power of the Lord was with them . . . many people were added to the Lord. . . . Then after further fasting and prayer they laid their hands on them and let them go." Note the message, the power, the many converts, and the sending forth of world missionaries. If they had been shaky and hesitant about the message there would have been no power, no converts, and no world mission. The message was the key: "the good news of Jesus Christ."

Let us go on with Hebrews 1:1-3: "Spoken to us in the Son whom he has made heir to the whole universe, and through whom he created all orders of existence." These two belong together, as effect and cause; he is heir to the whole universe because all orders of existence were created by Christ and for Christ and all in the end comes out at his feet—he is "heir" to all. That phrase "through whom he created all orders of existence" is one of the most important ever uttered. Along with other such passages such as these it becomes breathtaking: "And through him (Jesus Christ) all things came to be; no single thing was created without him. All that came to be was alive with his life" (John 1:3 NEB). Again: "In him (Jesus Christ) everything in heaven and on earth was created, not only things visible but also the invisible . . . the whole universe has been created through him and for him" (Col. 1:16 NEB). "In bringing many sons to glory, it was befitting that He for whom and by whom the universe exists. . . ." (Heb. 2:10 Moffatt.)

What do these amazing passages mean? If they mean any-thing it is that God created everything by Christ and for Christ; that everything in its inner structure is made to work in his way. When it works in his way it works well and when it works some other way it works its own ruin. The touch of Christ is upon all creation and this means not merely spirit but the whole being—body, mind, spirit, and relationships. This includes all creation: "For the created universe waits with eager expectation for God's sons to be revealed" (Rom. 8:19 NEB). For when the sons are revealed, the Christian purpose of creation is manifested; then lower nature will partake of that fulfillment.

These passages have been too great for the small hearts of Christendom. They passed them over as too good to be true. But a strange thing is happening: It is turning out to be a fact! The discoveries of science, psychology, sociology, and human experience are all converging on one thing: That everything in human life—individually and collectively, physically, men-tally, spiritually, and socially—works well in a Christian way and badly in some other way. When I say "a Christian way" I mean a Christlike way. That statement is the best corrob-orated fact in human history. As knowledge of how life works increases this is becoming increasingly evident. In another generation it will be a truism. Some day science is going to lay it all down on the table and say: "This is the way to live and this is the way not to live." We will look at these two lists and open our eyes with astonishment and exclaim: "Why, the way you say to live is the Christian way—every item is Christian. And the way you say not to live is the unchristian way." And they will probably reply: "About that conclusion we are not qualified to say, but this is the way life works and this is the way that life does not work!"

A clarification: I do not mean to say that living according to Christ is confined to those within the Christian church.

The Christian spirit has gone beyond the Christian church. I mean anyone anywhere, inside or outside the Christian church, who consciously or unconsciously lives according to Jesus Christ lives well and harmoniously with himself and others to the degree that he embodies the Christian way as seen in Jesus Christ.

The growing evidence: (1) William Sadler, the famous psychiatrist, says: "If people lived in a truly Christian way, half the diseases would drop off tomorrow morning and we would stand up, a new healthy race." (2) The head of a medical college said to me: "I've discovered the Kingdom of God at the end of my scalpel—it's in the tissues. The right thing morally, the Christian thing, is always the healthy thing physically." Then I replied: "Then the right thing morally, the Christian thing, is written not merely in the New Testament; it is also written in our tissues, our nerves, our organs, our relationships and therefore is inescapable. You can't jump out of your skin." He replied: "It's in the tissues. I've discovered it." And that discovery is as important as Harvey's discovery of circulation of the blood. And more important for the human race. (3) Alfred Adler, a famous psychiatrist, said: "I suppose all the ills of human personality can be traced back to not understanding the saying: 'It is more blessed to give than to receive.'" But Jesus said that two thousand years ago, and psychology after a lapse of centuries came across this saying and announced that if you don't know life according to this saying you don't know how to live. (4) When Dr. Kilpatrick, the educator, was asked, "What is the greatest discovery of modern education?" he replied: "The greatest discovery of modern education is: He that saveth his life shall lose it and he that loseth his life for a cause shall find it again." But Jesus used that sentence five times and in doing so lifted up the deepest law of the universe: Center yourself on yourself and you won't like yourself and nobody else will like you. Lose yourself in the cause of the Kingdom and you will find yourself released and happy and free to create! Now education comes along and says that that is our greatest discovery. It was not a discovery but a rediscovery of something written into reality and lifted up by Jesus. (5) Cancer cells are cells turned selfish. They refuse to serve the rest as the normal cells do, but make the rest serve them. So they eat their way to their own death and cause the death of the organism upon which they feed. They are cells turned pagan, antichristian. (6) A trapper, was shot through the stomach; when the wound healed an aperture was left so the doctors could look in and watch the process of digestion. When he was in a good humor and on good terms with everybody and himself, digestion was normal, the stomach blushed a rosy red, the gastric juices would flow down the walls of the stomach and the stomach would go into churning movements; digestion was normal. But the moment he became angry, the color of the stomach changed. The gastric juices ceased flowing and digestion was at an end. Evidently the stomach is made for goodwill, not ill will. In other words, you have a Christian stomach! Every organ of your body, every cell of your tissues, every part of your relationship with others works well in a Christian way and badly, or not at all, in an unchristian way.

"Food is meant for the stomach, and the stomach is meant for food. . . . The body is not made for immorality but for the Lord, and the Lord is for the body." (1 Cor. 6:13 Moffatt.) Here it specially says: "The body is made for the Lord"— made to work in his way and in no other way. And when it works in his way it works well and if it works in some other way it works its own ruin. In other words, your body is predestined to work in his way. You are structured for Christ. "Whom he did predestinate to be conformed to the image of his Son." (See Rom. 8:29.) I am predestined by my very makeup to be conformed to the image of his Son. I can live against that destiny for I am still free, but if I do I get hurt, automatically. Jesus said, "My meat is to do the will of him who sent me." God's will is my body's food. My will against God's will is my body's poison. Sin is poison. The word "evil" is the word "live" spelled backwards. The idea that you can have a good time in sin and evil is pure illusion. "It will keep the word of promise to your ear and break it to your hope." Carlyle said: "Sin is, has been, and ever shall be, the parent of misery." You cannot make it the parent of happiness. Nobody ever has, and nobody ever will.

A young man who was a Christian decided he would try to live life in another way, the unchristian way. So he did everything in the book that was evil. At the end of several years he said to a friend of mine: "Please help me to get back home." He was not at "home" in sin and evil; it was alien, anti-life. A Hindu young man said to me: "I went up the hill after committing adultery with a woman—I went up trembling." Why not singing? Sin and sadness are one and the same thing. The body is for the Lord and when you do the Lord's will you do the body's will, its deepest destiny. And "the Lord is for the body"; he is for its highest interest, its highest health, its happiness and well-being. He made it and he made it to work in his way.

An attractive young lady doctor, who had been having escapades with young men doctors and had been rationalizing it, was converted. She called up a friend and said: "I feel so clean this morning." Being a Christian was being clean, the opposite unclean.

I read somewhere if you change the secretions of a person's glands you can change his character, a good man will lose all moral sense and will swear like a trooper. I said to myself, "This is serious. Then morality must be in the glands and we had better go out and preach the gospel of good glands." I was nonplussed, until one day I asked a doctor if the state of mind and the emotions upset the secretion of glands. "They certainly do," he replied. "What states of mind and what kinds of emotions upset the secretion of glands?" I asked. He named them off. Everything he mentioned was unchristian. Light dawned. I asked him: "Suppose a person's glands were normal, suppose he lived in a truly Christian way, would his glands function well?" He replied: "They would function perfectly." Then I replied: "Then we have Christian glands." He replied: "I couldn't say anything against it."

I said to a hard-boiled newspaperman one day: "If you don't believe in the Christian way, why don't you go out and try it—put it under life and get the verdict of life. You go out and for a week say the unchristian thing, act the unchristian thing, think the unchristian thing, and do the unchristian thing in every situation. Then come back and tell me how you got on." He snorted: "Shucks, you would be bumped off before the end of the week." And I added, "Yes, and if someone didn't bump you off, you'd bump yourself off." For if you won't live with Christ, you can't live with yourself.

So when the statement is made in the passage under study: "Through whom he created all orders of existence," life as lived by trial and error is saying exactly the same thing. Life is rendering a verdict and it is a Christian verdict: Life works in his way and will not work in any other way.

So when the passage says: "But in this the final age he has spoken to us in the Son, whom he has made heir to the whole universe"—"made heir to the whole universe"? Arbitrarily? No factually. Everything is going to come out at his feet, or it won't come out, it will perish on the way. Is that wishful thinking, or is it factual observation? It is factual observation. Every revolt against Jesus Christ in human history, in the individual and in the collective, has turned out badly, is turning out badly, and will forever turn out badly.

Take a simple illustration: A Roman Catholic woman, the wife of a prominent doctor, came to our Ashram in spiritual and social trouble. Her husband was going around with another woman. She found Christ as the way out for her. She found resources in him to overcome her sorrow. She was happy. The husband kept asserting his "right to freedom." A friend of mine went to see this doctor on Sunday afternoon and found him pacing the floor with a whiskey bottle in one hand and tranquilizers in the other! That was his freedom—freedom to tie himself in knots, freedom to become a problem to himself and others. A whiskey bottle to buck him up and tranquilizers to tone him down. That's "freedom"?

That was personal, let us look at revolts on a world scale. When Woodrow Wilson at the Versailles Peace Conference was trying to remake a shattered world on the basis of goodwill, forgiveness, equal opportunity for all, Clemenceau, the Tiger, sneered and said, "Ah, Wilson talks like Jesus Christ." When the world began to go to pieces under the "revenge" attitudes of Clemenceau, built into the Treaty through his influence, Lloyd George sighed and said: "Would God that Wilson *had* talked like Jesus Christ, we wouldn't be in the increasing mess we are in." That "increasing mess" was a Second World War!

So individually and collectively everything must come out at the feet of Jesus; he must be "the heir of all things" or they will not come out at all, they will perish on the way. Every revolt in human history against Jesus Christ has turned out badly and sadly. Human experience as recorded in human history says a loud "Amen" to that statement. It echoes through the ages for those who have ears to hear and eyes to see.

Now look at two more characteristics of Jesus Christ as seen in this passage: "The Son who is the effulgence of God's splendor and the stamp of God's very being." This is startling: "The Son who is the effulgence of God's splendor," the Son who seen in the human perspective was the lowly One born in a stable, who worked at a carpenter's bench, washed his disciples' feet, came not to be served, but to serve and to give his life as a ransom; who was crucified between two thieves as one of them, and was laid in a borrowed tomb—he, "the effulgence of God's splendor?" "Effulgence" and "splendor" —do those fit God? Yes, for the God Jesus reveals is a serving, self-giving God; his "effulgence" is the effulgence of love, and the "splendor" or self-giving. "The Lamb who is at the heart of the throne," self-sacrifice is at the very heart of final power, the throne! Was there ever such a revelation of God? No one could have imagined that self-giving love was at the heart of power. That had to be revealed and revealed in a person, a self-giving person, a person on a cross. That is what Paul calls "the climax of history," and the climax of revelation.

This revelation could not be by a verbal description of the effulgence of God's splendor with a rainbow throne and Fourth of July fireworks around it. It had to be "the stamp of God's very being", had to be the revelation in himself of God's very being, the very essence of God's nature. And it is not something stamped *on* a paper, but it is the watermark *in* the paper. When you see Jesus you see the heart of ultimate reality. And nothing more beautiful has been or can be revealed, for there is nothing higher in God or man, nothing higher than self-giving love. For when you give yourself, your very self, in love, what more can you give? It is the ultimate of the ultimate. It is finality in the final.

Then comes the sequel of this love at the heart of the throne of the universe: "And sustains the universe by His word of power." Literally it could be translated "He holds together the universe by his word of power"—the power of love.

I write this in the heart of the Congo. During my visit several years ago the country was torn by internal strife. Rebels held this mission station captive. A missionary pilot, Burleigh Law, who came to rescue the women and children, was shot by a rebel soldier when he landed on the airstrip. His grave is a few feet from my window. I'm staying in the home of Paul Law, who has just come with his wife to take his father's place. Alongside Burleigh Law's grave is the grave of the Rev. Gonsalvo, who was the soul of an amazing revival among the

African villages. Whole villages and tribes were won over to
the Christian faith. Gonsalvo was the apostle of this awakening,
but he, too, died of internal injuries inflicted on him when
the rebels had charge. But his soul goes marching on. The
African superintendent who succeeded him told me today that
he had ten requests on his desk from pagan chiefs asking for a
"revival" in their villages. Those requests mean that the whole
village invites them to make them Christians. And not nominal
Christians but really converted Christians. Characters are
changed. A Roman Catholic official, a Belgian, reported: "It's
a moral movement. Crime goes down immediately, distillation
of illicit liquor stops, desire for education is awakened." The
whole village is turned inside out by the public confessionals
which last all night sometimes.

The point is that this mission station had been looted and
many Christians had had to flee to the jungle and stay there
in hiding four months, and now, by their reactions of love and
goodwill the people are asking to become Christians by whole
villages. In this sea of hate there were these islands of goodwill
and love. A foreigner said: "The Christians with their goodwill
held the Congo together." It would have gone down into chaos
had the Christians not held it together.

Every situation, individual and collective, where his spirit
is manifested, holds together; where that spirit is not present
it goes to pieces. No exceptions. Even the "God is dead" movement unwittingly acknowledged this because they were prepared to get along without God, but they were not prepared
to let Christ go; they said, "He is still alive in humanity," for
if he goes nothing would hold the universe together. He literally sustains the universe by his word of power—the power
of self-giving love.

As I sit here in the heart of the Congo in a place which
was a scene of riot and murder and hate, I remember how the
people had to hide in the jungles for fear of the rebels with
their hate and looting. I see that these same people now are

crowding the churches having been drawn together in love, and out of their grateful love, are offering themselves to Christ, literally by the hundreds. A Negro spiritual keeps singing its way through my mind and heart,

> Lift Him up, Lift Him up,
> Till He speaks from eternity:
> And I, if I be lifted up from the earth,
> Will draw all men unto Me.

Last night, so many crowded the altar of prayer for spiritual and physical healing that we were compelled to call it off, asking the remainder to stand *en masse* in the large church while we prayed for them all at once. "Love holds the world together." Love was holding the Congo together and healing its wounds.

I stood in the charred concrete church, a shell, in Hiroshima, Japan, a standing remnant with about six other buildings which survived the shock of the first atomic bomb. A city had been wiped out. At the close of my address the pastor, the Rev. Tanamoto, who had worked heroically rescuing the people, said: "A fire, the fire of love of the Holy Spirit has been kindled here this morning which will rebuild what the fire of the atomic bomb has destroyed." Love held that world together. The mayor of Hiroshima, at a luncheon, said, "If the sacrifices through which we have gone in Hiroshima could mean the end of war, we will gladly offer our sacrifices." Love was holding that world together.

I write this in the Fiji Islands where the people were cannibals. I saw yesterday the stone on which the skulls of the victims were bashed in including those of little children, preliminary to being eaten. That stone is now a baptismal font where babies and others are baptised. A church encloses it where cultured people, descendants of these cannibals, now sing the "Hallelujah Chorus" in marvellous harmony. Today

I saw a whale's tooth which when given to a man bound him to kill a man. Now a whale's tooth is presented in a quarrel, and if one or the other receives it, the quarrel ends. The whale's tooth which fomented hate now forbids it. It holds that world together. The hollow log which when beaten called the tribe to war, now when beaten calls the people to church —converted it holds that world together in love.

We come now to the last item of this amazing seven-fold description of Jesus Christ and what he does: "When he brought about the purgation of sins, he took his seat at the right of majesty on high." The climax of all he was and did was: "He brought about the purgation of sins"; or as Moffatt puts it, "When he had secured our purification of sins." That was the climax of his work, to secure "purification of our sins." Was that climax an anticlimax? No, for the greatest need of humanity is "the purification of our sins." Beside this need all other needs are marginal, this is central. For all the problems of humanity come out of one thing: sin. Is that old fashioned? Then so be it. But it is true and relevant. I have studied the vast misery of the world, North, East, South, and West for over a half century, and in every situation without exception, the person concerned or the group concerned, somebody has sinned or is sinning. "The wages of sin is death"— decay, misery.

When they named Jesus they said: "Thou shalt call his name Jesus for he shall save his people from their sins"—not in their sins, but from. They put their finger on the central business of his coming, not to save from hell or to heaven, but to save them from their sins. The last thing the writer of Hebrews said he is to do before sitting down at the right hand of God was "to make purification of sins." So first and last he was a savior from sin. And there is nothing, absolutely nothing, that this age needs so much as to be saved from their sins; for individual and collective sin is the basic reason for all our problems. We have wasted billions of words in analyzing our individual and world problems and they could all be reduced to one word—sin!

So Jesus stands in the midst of a baffled world, dealing with symptoms, and puts his finger on the disease. Moreover, he does not end in analysis, he ends in an accomplished fact; he "had made purification of our sins." So if we accept him and follow him we are free from the central and fatal illness of our age. That makes the rest of the so-called saviors of humanity, secular and religious, look like dabblers and it makes Jesus the deliverer. He is at the right hand of power for that is where he belongs. Jesus is Lord!

So when the persecuted disciples preached "the good news of Jesus Christ" they put their finger on the basic need of this age: It needs to hear the "good news of Jesus Christ" and not "good views about Jesus Christ." One is moonlight and the other is sunlight! So when pessimism sadly says, "Put out the candles lightning has struck the world," Christian faith gladly says, "Put out the candles, the Sun is up." Jesus is alive. And "Jesus is Lord," not will be Lord, but *is* Lord, at the right hand of final authority, and he will have the last word in human affairs; whoever has the first word or the intermediate word, he will have the last word. "I am the Omega."

So in the reconstructed church we will make the basis "the good news of Jesus Christ," for when the scattered disciples did this at Antioch, "the strong hand of the Lord was upon them and many people were added to the Lord." We will turn a deaf ear to those who counsel that we leave out "God" and "Christ" in order to have a more unobstructed approach to the modern man. I have heard of two suggestions of this kind, one from the head of a group movement and the other from a visitor to the members of a board of evangelism of a great denomination—they both advocated leaving out "God" and "Christ" and talking about the "good life." If God and Christ go what have you got left? Nothing but a humanism. Then the passage would read: "They preached good views about the good life and the weak hand of humanism was upon them and nobody was added to the Lord."

Moreover, we will repudiate the attempt to win people by being like them. We will maintain a "core of difference," for that difference will make people want to be different. This trying to win people by being like them came to the ultimate absurdity in a young man, a part of a group of young men, sent to the Congo from the West to serve. He put beer bottles in his front window to let the people know he was one of them. No wonder the African bishop bundled him off to America. The youth complained that he couldn't see why he was being sent home, for he had been told before he came "not to conform to the system." This beer-bottle, cigarette-smoking, swearing nonconformity is a dead failure, for the people see through it—they have nothing but nonconformity. We are to conform to Jesus Christ, the Universal Man, then we are universal, at home anywhere, with anybody, anywhere. Every dimming emphasis on Jesus Christ has meant decay. Every rediscovery of Jesus Christ has meant revival—of God, of the Kingdom, of everything.

The way back to reconstruction is to begin where Antioch began; it began with "the good news of Jesus Christ." Everything else followed when they followed through on that basis. It wasn't everything, so just to rediscover "the good news of Jesus Christ," will not solve everything, but it was the basis of everything. It had to be worked out in all relationships, personal and social. It was. The church became a *Christian* church with Jesus Christ inspiring and working out its relationships. He was the pattern. He was the goal, and he was the dynamic moving on to that goal.

But while the good news of Jesus Christ was the basis it was linked with "the good news of the Kingdom of God." Here I must recapitulate what I emphasized in the opening of this book—the Gospel of the Kingdom. "The Gospel of the Kingdom of God" is the only thing Jesus ever called his Gospel.

He sent out his disciples to "preach the gospel of the Kingdom." He used interchangeably "for my sake" and "for the Kingdom's sake." Was he the Kingdom embodied? Then that is important, for if that is so then it makes our Christian faith at once individual and at once social. For if you have personal relationships with Jesus you have personal relationships with that Kingdom embodied in him. But that Kingdom is both personal and social. The entrance into that Kingdom is personal and by a new birth. "Except a man be born again he cannot see the Kingdom of God." "Except ye be converted and become as little children you cannot enter the Kingdom of God." But while the entrance is personal, the nature of that Kingdom is social. It is God's absolute order, demanding a total obedience in the total life. It demands that the inmost thought come under the sway of the Kingdom, and it goes out to the outmost rim of social relationships and demands that they be brought under the sway of the Kingdom: "The Kingdom of God shall be taken away from you and given to a nation that shall bring forth the fruits thereof." The nation as a corporate entity is to bring forth the fruits of the Kingdom.

The Gospel of the person of Jesus and the Gospel of the Kingdom viewed as one puts together the individual and the social. We need both. An individual gospel without a social gospel is a soul without a body, and a social gospel without an individual gospel is a body without a soul. One is a ghost and the other is a corpse. You can take your choice. I don't want one or the other. I want both. The ghost and the corpse coming together makes a living person.

This fits in with the New Testament emphasis: "But when they came to believe Philip with his good news about the kingdom of God and the name of Jesus Christ, they were baptised, men and women alike" (Acts 8:12 NEB). Again: "He spoke urgently of the kingdom of God and sought to convince them about Jesus" (Acts 28:23 NEB) ; "He stayed there full two years . . . proclaiming the kingdom of God and teaching the facts about the Lord Jesus Christ" (Acts 28:30, 31 NEB). So there was a double emphasis in the Acts: Jesus Christ and the Kingdom of God, the absolute person and the absolute order—the unchanging person, "Jesus Christ the same yesterday, today and forever," and the unshakable Kingdom,—"Let us be thankful that we receive a Kingdom which cannot be shaken." (See Heb. 13:8; 12:28.)

With these two things we must confront this confused age: the unshakable Kingdom and the unchanging Person. The absolute that lays its hand upon the individual will and says: "Repent, submit, surrender, be converted, and obey," and lays its hand upon the collective will and says: "Repent, submit, surrender, be converted, and obey." And to both we can say with absolute assurance: "This is your freedom. For this is a totalitarianism, which when totally obeyed allows total freedom." This is a vital difference between man's earthborn totalitarianisms, fascism, nazism, and communism—which if totally obeyed, produce total bondage.

In a similar crisis period this is the point at which the church took a wrong turning. At the World Missionary Conference in Madras, in 1938, when the earthborn totalitarianisms were arising, I begged the Conference to confront them with God's absolute, the unshakable Kingdom of God. They refused and chose the ecumenical church instead. (I believe in the ecumenical church. I have given my life, my endeavors for over a half century to produce it, but the ecumenical church is not the answer.) The ecumenical church is a relativism, related to something higher than itself, the Kingdom of God. To confront relativisms with another relativism is bad strategy and bound to fail. Suppose we go out and say to the world: "Repent for the ecumenical church is at hand." They would laugh, as my audiences do laugh when I make the suggestion. But when I say: "Repent for the Kingdom of God is at hand," you don't laugh, you bend the knee, if you have any sense. The church's confusion and comparative impotence in this confused and groping age is because it has lost its absolute, the unshakable Kingdom. So it offers half answers—secularize, withdraw, this marginal thing, that marginal thing, this doubt, that doubt. The world shrugs its burdened shoulders and says: "You are as confused as we are; two confusions don't make a solution."

I was in a ministers' retreat and I taught the ministers about the "Three Finger Greeting and Farewell." The oldest Christian creed was three words: "Jesus is Lord." "If thou wilt confess with thy mouth 'Jesus is Lord' . . . thou shalt be saved. No man can say 'Jesus is Lord' except by the Holy Spirit." In both places the phrase "Jesus is Lord" is in quotation marks showing it was used as an early Christian confession, perhaps the earliest Christian creed. So we've adopted those three words and made them into three fingers—"Jesus is Lord." It is a reduction of the Christian faith into three words. It is used widely as a Christian greeting. The last thing I saw of Dr. Brunner, the Swiss theologian, was him standing on a veranda in Japan and putting up his three fingers in answer to ours as we got into a car. And the last thing I saw of the Congo Christians as we said goodbye last night was the Three Fingers. And the last gift we had from them was an African boy carved in ivory holding up his three fingers. They end the services in many parts of the Congo with the three fingers.

The ministers' conference mentioned above gave the salutation of the three fingers as we said goodnight. But the next morning a young minister at breakfast said: "I held up my three fingers last night and said 'Jesus is Lord' with the rest. But I've just come out of the seminary where there is a fashionable word prevalent, 'perhaps,' so under my breath I said, 'Jesus is Lord, perhaps.' " The paralysis of "perhaps" is the most paralyzing element upon the preaching of the present.

There is a reaction, a redemptive reaction is taking place. "Perhaps preaching" is a paralyzed preaching—a paralysis for the preacher and a paralysis for the expectant audience. It has had its day and the day has ended in a dull sunset. "Put out the candles, the Sun is up!" "Jesus is Lord"—unqualified and unequivocal. We need to have our question marks straightened out into exclamation points. "Jesus is Lord!"

I saw the original document in London of the articles which founded the YMCA, drawn up in the handwriting of George Williams, the founder. At the top the original said: "Young Men's Religious Association." That word "Religious," was crossed out and "Christian" was inserted above it. I have called that line that crossed out "Religious" and put in "Christian" as the most important short line drawn in history. If the YMCA had been vaguely religious, instead of vitally Christian and drawing its substance and its vitality and redemption from the person of Christ, it would have died of that vagueness. Now it lives on to the degree that it is "Christian." Many of our churches are vaguely religious, instead of being vitally Christian —and they are growingly empty.

The Antioch church, without mention of the building in which it met, becomes the pattern of the building of the reconstructed Church, because it revealed the heart of the Christian movement, its vitality and universality, because it was thoroughly Christian. "The disciples were first called Christians at Antioch." You don't have to become less Christian to be universal, you have to become more. For the Christian faith is the good news of the one universal God, revealed in the universal Man, and presenting the universal Kingdom, founded on universal principles, and offered to universal man.

XV

WHAT ABOUT THE UNITY
OF THE CHURCHES?

Because the kind of unity which I believe in is not specifically mentioned in Antioch, my first draft of this manuscript left it out. But now I am putting it in, for necessity demands it. To talk about the reconstruction and leave out its fundamental structure is to leave out its central necessity. For the structure of the Christian churches is fundamentally unchristian—it is competitive, not cooperative. So the church of the future must be cooperative, not here and there on the edges, but basically so if it is to be a Christian church. To be a Christian church there must be one church; now we have a multiplicity of churches. The church at Antioch has the seeds of a united church in it and of a universally united church.

They looked on the church at Jerusalem as one of them —they called them "fellow-Christians." "So the disciples agreed to make a contribution, each according to his means, for the relief of their fellow-Christians in Judaea." (Acts 11:29 NEB.)

The church in Jerusalem felt an organic connection with the church at Antioch, so when "the news reached the ears of the church in Jerusalem . . . they sent Barnabas to Antioch. When he arrived and saw the divine grace at work, he rejoiced, and encouraged them all to hold fast to the Lord with resolute hearts; for he was a good man, full of the Holy Spirit and of faith. And large numbers were won over to the Lord" (Acts 11:22-24 NEB). They sent Barnabas, not to direct the church in the name of the Jerusalem church, but to be associated with a movement which was under the direction of the Holy Spirit. It was a unity with freedom. Barnabas didn't refer the question of getting Paul associated with Antioch—he went off on the impulse of the Spirit to look for Paul and brought him to Antioch. When the church worshiped the Lord and heard the voice of the Spirit saying: "Separate me Barnabas and Saul for the work to which I have called them," they didn't say, "Well, we had better refer this to Jerusalem to get their consent and guidance." They didn't, instead the account says: "Then after further fasting and prayer they laid their hands on them and let them go. So those two sent out on their mission by the Holy Spirit came down to Seleucia."

Here was an organic union of churches, so organic that when Jerusalem suffered they suffered with them and sent them relief "according to each one's ability"; and they accepted Jerusalem's oversight and guidance in the person of Barnabas. They acknowledged they were organically connected with the church at Jerusalem. And yet they were free, free to create, free to bring Paul in as a guest of the church for a year, free to send Paul and Barnabas on a world mission, free to lay their hands on them in commission without asking that Jerusalem's hands be laid on them. And they laid their hands on the emissary from Jerusalem instead of that emissary, Barnabas, laying hands on them.

Here was union with freedom—one with Jerusalem and freedom to do as the Spirit directed apart from Jerusalem. If this teaches us anything it teaches that the disciples were Christian when they were organically connected with all other Christians and free to obey the guidance of the Spirit, free to create.

If it teaches us anything it teaches us that the present compartmentally divided state of Christendom, each walled off from the rest by denominational walls, feeling and acting and re-acting denominationally is sub-Christian and often anti-Christian. "Everyone who belongs to Christ, belongs to everyone who belongs to Christ." That is basic and fundamental. But there is something else just as fundamental: That belonging to another group must not be so constrictive that creation is impossible. They must be free to create.

What pattern of church union would fit that pattern of union with freedom? It would be federal union.

There are four patterns possible for the union of the churches: First, union through councils of churches. Second, union through federation of churches. Third, union through mergers of churches. Fourth, union through federal union.

Union through councils of churches is good, but not good enough. The councils are councils to separate, sovereign denominations. The area of their work is cooperation but not union. We must go beyond cooperation to union. Federation is a step beyond the councils, but is this side of union. The federating denominations are intact, surrendered to nothing beyond themselves, but are federating to do certain things together. It is the position of the Colonies when they had "Articles of Confederation" among themselves. But while this existed for ten years, it broke down, the tensions within broke it down, and they had to go beyond federation to federal union to save the union. The United States of America is not a federation, but a federal union.

The third is merger. Suppose the Colonies had said: "The way to union is uniformity. We will wipe out these Colonies, their names, their identities, their boundaries and we will merge them into one state, ruled from Washington." How far would they have gone with that proposal? I asked that question in Texas. They burst out laughing. For Texas is a state of mind. I asked it in Rhode Island and they, too, burst out laughing. From the biggest to the smallest it would have been absurd. Our fathers were wiser: they said "Come in with your names, identities, your boundaries, and we will have a union of diversity. We will have a federal union." We became perhaps the most united peoples of the world, because we put together two apparently opposite necessities of human nature— a desire for union with the whole and a desire for local freedom; union with freedom came together in a living blend. Merger satisfies the desire for union with the whole, but it constricts and chokes the local desire for freedom to create.

So every merger has resulted in a static union with little or no sense of creation, its energies exhausted with problems of accommodation with each other, the merging bodies. It has been so in Japan in the Kyodan, where the bodies staying out of the union have maintained and increased their creative activities and initiative, lacking in the Kyodan. Recently with fifteen thousand congregations and pastors the Kyodan increased their total membership a few hundred in a year. The same with the South India United Church, begun with great expectancy and continuing with increasing problems, court cases over inner tensions instead of evangelism resulting in extensions. The United Church of Canada has lost its drive. A United Church pastor told of one ex-alcoholic who is winning more people to Christ in a year than the whole of the United Church. Exaggerated? Possibly, but indicative of a sloweddown, sterile union.

The open possibility is federal union. Applied to the churches what would it mean? "An outline for a Constitution of a United Church in America"—and the world—would be as follows:

The name of the united church: "The Church of Jesus Christ in America." (Note: It would not be a state church "of America," but a part of the universal church; "The Church of Jesus Christ," but located "in America.")

This united church would be a *Christian* church—"The Church of Jesus Christ," with him as the center of its loyalty.

He is our starting point, our Alpha; he is our ending point, our Omega. Through him we see and find God; through him we see and find the Kingdom of God; in him we find our redemption, individual and collective, and in him we find our power to live now.

Since Jesus Christ is the center of the union, then the central confession of our faith would be the confession that Peter made and Jesus approved, and is the "rock" upon which the church is to be built: "Jesus is the Christ the Son of the living God." Any branch that will make that confession is on the "rock." (Some would prefer the three historic creeds—the Nicean, the Athanasian, the Apostles'—as the basis of union. We would not object to that. But if we take the confession that "Jesus is the Christ, the Son of the living God," we simplify the basis of the union. Yet we leave open to any branch to add more than this central confession as an expression of its own faith. But the basis of admission into the union would be this basic confession: "Jesus is the Christ, the Son of the living God.")

This union would be called a branch union. Since Jesus said: "I am the vine, ye are the branches," we could change the "vine" into a tree without change of meaning. The root of the tree is God; the trunk is Jesus Christ; the various churches are the branches. All the branches inhere in the trunk and find their source of sustenance and union in him. Since branches of a tree are different in form, but all find their union in the trunk, so the branches of union will be different, frankly so, but out of the very differences will form a symmetrical whole. The union will not be a union of compromise, but a union of comprehension.

There will be one church: "The Church of Jesus Christ in America"; but under it there will be branches. That transition from "churches" to "branches" of the one church is decisive. That makes branch union go beyond councils and federations, which leave the bodies involved separate and sovereign and surrendered to nothing beyond themselves. This plan makes them a union; the union is supreme and sovereign under Jesus Christ the head.

So in branch union there would be branches under the union: "The Lutheran Branch of the Church of Jesus Christ in America"; "The Baptist Branch"; "The Episcopal Branch"; "The Nazarene Branch"; "The Church of God Branch"; "The United Church of Christ Branch"; "The Presbyterian Branch"; "The United Methodist Branch"; "The Salvation Army Branch"; etc.

Within those branches there would be local self-government, states rights. If any branch would desire and require adult baptism by immersion they would be free to do so within the branch, but they would not compel others to do the same as the price of union. If any branch should desire to have bishops they could have them, and they could function within that branch and that branch could look on them as they liked, but again, they would not require the rest to accept bishops as the price of union. Branch union is a union of diversity.

The proposed union would be an organic union. It could act as a single organism. The United States of America is an organic union; it is a single organism and can act as such. This differentiates it from a council of states or a federation of states—it is a *federal union of states*. The union is sovereign and supreme. So branch union is not a council of churches, whose area is cooperation not union, nor a federation of churches, whose function is to federate to do certain things together, but each federating body is still separate and sovereign and surrendered to nothing but itself. In branch union the union is sovereign, but with states rights. Both merger and branch union want organic union—one with a monolithic structure, the other with a federal structure, and union with freedom under that union.

Branch union puts together two apparently contradictory urges: (1) the desire for union with the whole; and (2) the desire for local self-government, local freedom. It puts together union with freedom. Merger fulfills one urge, desire for union with the whole; but it provides little or no freedom under it. What we now have in separate denominationalism gives freedom, but little or no sense of union. Branch union puts together the two urges into a living blend.

Moreover, while branch union fulfills these two urges it also fulfills the prayer of Jesus, as the head of the church: "I will that they may be one as we are one." How is God one? One undifferentiated being? No. There is the Father, the Son, and the Holy Spirit—each with a name, each with a function, each with a separate identity, and yet profoundly one, union in diversity. He prays that we may be one "as we are one." That points to some form of branch union, a union in diversity.

Over these branches there will be a "General Assembly of the Church of Jesus Christ in America." This would be the sovereign body, the total church in action authoritatively. The General Assembly would have to do with everything that has to do with the total church: (1) a strategy for evangelism, for education, for missions at home and abroad; (2) a strategy and program for social reconstruction at home and abroad; (3) the relationship of branch with branch; (4) all other subjects assigned to it by a Constitutional Convention; (5) the residue of subjects such as theological education, would remain in the branch assemblies, except where by mutual consent of the branches concerned. Seminaries and other institutions could be amalgamated.

The general assembly would be constituted of representatives, appointed or elected by the various branches. If so decided by the Constitutional Convention, there could be two houses—one made up of equal representatives, say two, from each of the branches, and another house made up of representatives from the branches according to numbers.

Under the general assembly there would be a state assembly, a county assembly, a city assembly, a town assembly.

In these local assemblies the question of overlapping, competition, duplication, could be dealt with. The Christian movement could be streamlined for its local and world tasks. (Note: It may be objected that the use of state assembly is not the same in political division and in denominational division— one is geographical and the other is denominational and this goes beyond geographical boundaries. But in both cases, while the state is used as a convenient entity, nevertheless the actual division is psychological, which goes beyond state boundaries. For instance, states are ruled by Republican Parties or Democrat Parties, which are psychological and go beyond state boundaries. In the branch union plan also we would use the state boundary for convenience, the psychological factor in the branches would be the directing force.)

Each nation can have its own national expression of "The Church of Jesus Christ." "The Church of Jesus Christ in Britain"; "The Church of Jesus Christ in Scandinavia"; "The Church of Jesus Christ in Germany"; "in Africa"; "in India"; "in Japan"; and so forth. They would be national expressions of the one universal church. Each national genus would be free to express itself in its own way, but be a part of the total church.

There would be a world assembly of the "Church of Jesus Christ of the World" made up of the representatives of the various national assemblies of the world. Here the total Christian church of the world could speak and act authoritatively. Suppose it could speak now, would the nations listen? They would have to, for the Christian church of the world holds the largest single allegiance around a single loyalty, that loyalty around Jesus Christ as Lord.

Moreover, the Christian church holds sixty-two percent of the population of the United States, the largest single allegiance around a single loyalty of any group. Would its moral and spiritual influence be felt if we could speak as one? The question answers itself. (Note: If we are true to our faith our influence would be exerted on the nation in these words: "He who would be greatest among you shall be the servant of all." Our greatness would be in our "service" to society.)

The present council of churches on the local, state, national, and world level, or local federation of churches, or other bodies representing local interests, could be revamped and made into executives of the "Church of Jesus Christ" in their various levels. They would be changed from councils to executives.

In regard to the property, it would be held as now by the branches. Only that property would be held by the union which would be created by or given to the union.

There would be little property upset, but a great deal of property saving as duplications and overlapping would be done away and the church streamlined for its local and world tasks.

Under branch union, if two or more branches should desire to merge they could do so. There would be that many fewer branches in "The Church of Jesus Christ in America." So union by merger could go on under branch union as far as it is considered desirable to do so. Its limitations are obvious. (Note: But branch union cannot go on under merger; so branch union is a more comprehensive proposal than merger.)

In regard to the recognition of ministries and members, there would be a great service of mutual recognition of members and ministries by giving each other the right hand of fellowship. This was done when the two branches of the Christian church came together in the persons of Paul and the Jerusalem Apostles. Neither was called on to bend the knee in submission to the other or to be ordained by the other, but both stood face to face, equal before God and therefore equal before each other, and by giving "the right hand of fellowship" the two branches were made one, and ministries and members recognized. (Note: This would obviate the unreal and less-than-honest proposal of a mutual laying on of hands, which would not be "mutual," for it would mean one thing to one group—apostolic succession—and something else to another group—recognition.) This would have a basic dishonesty and unreality at its inception. But mutual recognition by the right hand of fellowship would be completely honest and honorable. Probably ninety percent could give the right hand of fellowship straight off. We would leave the remaining ten percent to time and the Spirit of God. Things are moving and walls are falling. In the meantime, we could take the hesitant ten percent into the union in an associate membership).

In regard to the Roman Catholic Church, we would take the attitude that if the Roman Catholic Church would confess that "Jesus is the Christ, the Son of the living God," and that they are a branch, and we as Protestants are branches, then there would be a "Roman Catholic Branch of the Church of Jesus Christ in America." The door is open to everybody on that condition. (Note: If the pattern of union among Protestants should be merger, when we come to the final union between Protestants and Roman Catholics, would we merge and become Roman Catholics, or would the Roman Catholics merge and become Protestants? Both are unthinkable. Branch union is a consistant plan which could be used in the initial and in the final stages.)

When branch union was put up to the Patriarch of the Greek Orthodox Church and his clergy in Jerusalem, he commented: "Very good, but who would be at the head of it?" The reply: "Jesus Christ is the head of the church. But in the structure of the branches of the church, in the state, general and world Assemblies, a Roman Catholic representative will preside one year, a Greek Orthodox representative the next year, and a Protestant the third year. There would be rotation." His reply: "That would be all right then."

Since merger, wherever tried, in Japan, Canada, South India, has resulted, not in revival and renewal, as expected, but in a slowed-down, nonvitalized type of church life, it will probably do so again, if tried in America. The drive in the branches would be gone. But in branch union we would harness the drive of the branches to the collective good. Now the drive is competitive, then it will be cooperative, but the drive will still be there. The branch union will have a corporate drive and an individual drive, both working toward the same ends.

Moreover, branch union would mean that practically all the denominations would come in. It would give us a sense of solidarity which we do not have now and would not have if merger is insisted on as the plan of union. For after years of negotiations, of debate, and compromises in endeavoring to have a merger, the result will be a merger of some churches, but this would not be church union. It would be a union of some churches. Branch union would be church union.

I believe that the adoption of branch union will have the people of our churches behind it. For the people want union but they want to keep their heritages. Branch union will give them union and will allow them to keep their heritages. It gives union with freedom.

If the objection is raised that while we object to remaking the church after the pattern of the secular city, we are actually proposing the adoption of federal union as the pattern of church unity, which is the very structural essence of the secular state, the reply is that this passage is the center of federal union: "To make peace by the creation in himself of a new man out of both parties." (See Eph. 2:15.) To create a new man out of both parties is to get both parties to change and come to something higher than each, but gathering up the good of each. This is the very center of the federal principle. It was embodied in the Christian outlook and practise before it was adopted by the secular state. It is a universal principle —marriage is a federal union, one name and yet each with his or her own name, a union of persons and yet each has his or her own person. It is the deepest and most lasting and most effective kind of union there is. Merger is built up;

federal union is built in. Merger expresses the contrivance of man; federal union expresses the principle on which the universe is built. One works with the grain of the universe —the other works against it.

"Jesus is Lord."